PEARL HARBOR:
THE CONTINUING CONTROVERSY

By

Hans L. Trefousse

AN ANVIL ORIGINAL
under the general editorship of
LOUIS L. SNYDER

ROBERT E. KRIEGER PUBLISHING COMPANY
MALABAR, FLORIDA
1982

Printed and Published by
ROBERT E. KRIEGER PUBLISHING COMPANY, INC.
KRIEGER DRIVE
MALABAR, FLORIDA 32950

Printed in the United States of America

Library of Congress Cataloging in Publication Data

Trefousse, Hans Louis.
    Pearl Harbor, the continuing controversy.

    (An Anvil original, ISSN 0570-1062)
    Bibliography: p.
    Includes index.
    1. Pearl Harbor, Attack on, 1941. I. Title.
D767.92T69   940.54'26   81-14237
ISBN 0-89874-261-7   AACR2

To the Memory of
John A. Carpenter

TABLE OF CONTENTS

INTRODUCTION

At 7:55 a.m. on Sunday, December 7, 1941, Japanese carrier-borne aircraft attacked the American fleet at Pearl Harbor. Eight battleships, three cruisers, three destroyers, and four other ships, eighteen in all, were sunk or severely damaged, over two thousand lives and almost two hundred planes lost, and the American fleet in the Pacific temporarily disabled. The nation was stunned. Its friends were incredulous and the Japanese jubilant.

Yet the attackers had little reason for their elation. At one stroke, they had solved President Franklin D. Roosevelt's most difficult problem, a conundrum with which he had been wrestling for over a year, how to overcome the isolationist opposition to American aid to Great Britain in its struggle against Nazi Germany. The attack on Pearl Harbor and on other American installations in the Pacific unified the American people overnight. When Germany and Italy declared war a few days later, they merely strengthened America's resolve, and the end result was the total defeat of the Axis powers. Japan's decision to strike at the American fleet was an even more fateful Axis blunder than Hitler's previous assault on the Soviet Union.

In the years since the attack, the story of Pearl Harbor and of America's final entry into the Second World War has been told over and over again, and almost from the first, a serious controversy developed. Who was responsible for the disaster? Could it have been averted? And was it not strange that the President's political difficulties were resolved by a Japanese assault? To these questions, many different answers have been given, largely favorable to the administration by those who tend to sympathize with its handling of foreign policy, and unfavorable by those critical of it. The latter, often former isolationists, were naturally benumbed at first. Their previous objections to American involvement in war seemed out of date, and further opposition downright treasonable. Yet they were by no means satisfied. As time went on, too many unexplained facts about the attack came to light. How much of a surprise had it really been? What possible provocation had caused the Japanese to undertake so rash a venture? Why were the commanding officers at Hawaii, Admiral Husband E. Kimmel and General Walter C. Short, admittedly able commanders, taken unaware, and why were they retired soon after the disaster under such peculiar circumstances? Perhaps there was more to the incident than met the eye, a theory John T. Flynn and William Neumann propounded as early as 1944. And when a series of investigations revealed that American intelligence had broken the most secret Japanese government codes, a process called *Magic,* these suspicions were heightened. Was it not amazing that a country that was able to decipher Japanese espionage messages about the exact disposition of the fleet at Pearl Harbor and the imminent break in relations between Tokyo and Washington was taken completely by surprise on Pearl Harbor day? And was it not even more amazing that, duly warned, responsible officials in Washington failed properly to alert the commanders in the field?

Further revelations merely increased the skepticism of Roosevelt's critics. It appeared that General George C. Marshall, the Chief of Staff, instead of being doubly on the alert on December 7, was taking a long, leisurely horseback ride through the Virginia countryside just as the crucial warning messages were coming in. It also turned out that Admiral Harold R. Stark, the Chief of Naval Operations, at first refused to take any action in response to these intercepts and then only reluctantly agreed to a final alert. And it appears that when Marshall at length did return to his office, he sent warning messages to the commanders of American units in the Pacific but failed to ensure their prompt delivery, so that the one destined for Hawaii was transmitted by commercial cable and arrived only after the bombs had already fallen. Perhaps all the talk of surprise was a blind; perhaps Roosevelt, in a gigantic plot, had been manipulating events all along.

In time, these suspicions ripened into conviction. Charles A. Beard, Harry Elmer Barnes, Charles C. Tansill,

6

Admiral Kimmel, Robert A. Theobald, Kemp Tolley, and their supporters became certain that the hard-pressed President, unable to induce the United States to enter the war in the Atlantic, finally decided to do so via the "back door" in the Pacific. In order to persuade the Japanese to attack, some argued, Roosevelt based his fleet on Pearl Harbor, goaded Tokyo to desperation by refusing to lift an oil embargo, and withheld vital information from his own admirals and generals so that their actions would not alert a potential enemy. This scenario, sensational in its implications, became the theme of the revisionist historians. If it was sometimes modified by references to three small vessels the President sent out from Manila allegedly to provoke an attack—the idea that he would willingly sacrifice the entire Pacific fleet was too difficult to believe—the notion of a conspiracy remained at the heart of the anti-Roosevelt school's hypothesis. Leading participants, anxious to set the record straight, have repeatedly written and testified about such peculiar occurrences as the receipt in Washington of messages to Japanese agents requesting minute information about the location of ships at Pearl Harbor, intercepts that were not forwarded to the Commander of the Pacific fleet. Others have concentrated upon the alledged arrival of a so-called Winds-Execute signal, a secret code set up by the Japanese to warn of the imminence of a break with the United States. Repeated over and over again, the conspiracy theory has found a degree of acceptance, even though no conclusive evidence to substantiate it has ever come to light.

It is natural that postwar developments contributed to the persistence of the controversy. At a time when the United States was engaged in a struggle with the Soviet Union all over the world, many observers naturally questioned the wisdom of the wartime alliance with Russia. Yet, not even the lessening of the Cold War in the seventies brought a respite from the arguments about Pearl Harbor. The controversy has continued to flourish as it did for the previous thirty years. Perhaps the following recapitulation and the accompanying documents may contribute to a better understanding of the circumstances leading up to America's final entry into the Second World War.

Part I

PEARL HARBOR: THE CONTINUING
CONTROVERSY

CHAPTER ONE

BACKGROUND

When on March 4, 1933, Franklin D. Roosevelt became President of the United States, foreign affairs were
not his primary concern. Faced with the most far-reaching
depression in history, he utilized all his energies to effect a
revival of the economy, to restore confidence, and to put
Americans back to work. Yet the world situation could
not be ignored. A few weeks earlier, Adolf Hitler had
become Chancellor in Germany, and Japan, determined
to carry out its expansionist policy by force, was about to
leave the League of Nations. For the United States, like
Great Britain and France one of the beneficiaries of the
international realignment following the First World War,
threats to world peace were ominous. And developments
in both Germany and Japan clearly indicated that these
forebodings were very real.

German Threats to the United States. The coming
to power of Hitler and his Nazi party was a matter of
great concern for the United States. As the world's leading
democracy, America could not view with equanimity a
regime that publicly announced its disdain for free institutions, a government that ridiculed the parliamentary
system, denounced free elections, rejected religious tol-
erance, and deliberately sought to substitute a war-like
dictatorship for accustomed forms of popular rule. Within
a short time, Hitler and his cohorts began to make good
their boasts. Abolishing the Weimar Republic, they established a one-party system, curtailed and eventually ended
all civil liberties, persecuted Jews and other dissidents, and
began to rearm. Thus they not only challenged the idea of
democracy but were well on the way to upsetting the
existing balance of power in Europe. When in 1936 they
concluded the so-called Anti-Comintern Pact, pledging
cooperation with Japan, allegedly against communism,
but in reality against the Soviet Union, they served notice
on the world that they were ready to make common cause

with the ever more militaristic island empire. In addition, they introduced unorthodox trading methods in their attempt to create economic autarchy. Instituting a transfer moratorium applicable to all foreign debts, they caused serious misgivings in the United States, where 40 percent of that debt was held. They granted indirect subsidies to exports and materially interfered with German-American trade relations at a time when the United States was interested in expanding reciprocal trade agreements. Economic relations between the two countries became even more strained when in 1935 the 1923 German-American Treaty of Friendship with its most-favored-nation clause expired. It did not improve matters that the Third Reich also began to compete with the United States in Latin America.

Japanese Threats to the United States. While Germany was falling victim to Hitlerism, Japan was also turning toward government by force. Overawed by an ever more aggressive military clique, the civilian leaders of the Empire were living under constant threats of assassination. Their freedom of action severely restricted, they experienced real difficulty in satisfying both their military critics and the needs of their people. If this situation brought them into collision with foreign countries, there was little they could do about it. Japanese expansion, a perpetual demand of the military, was bound to conflict with established American interests in the Far East. This became evident in 1931 when Imperial troops conquered Manchuria and even more so in 1937 after the beginning of the so-called "China Incident," Japan's attempt to take over all of China by force. Committed to the maintenance of an independent and friendly Chinese government and the preservation of its territorial integrity in accordance with the principles of the Open Door as expressed in the Nine-Power Pact, the United States could not simply fail to take notice of the Japanese penetration of the country.

The United States and the Coming of the War in Europe. With the passing of time, it became more and more evident that the post-war order in the Old World was collapsing. In October 1933, Germany left the League. In March 1935, she announced the introduction of conscription in violation of the Treaty of Versailles, and in October, Italy invaded Ethiopia. In 1936, German troops reoccupied the Rhineland in contravention not only of the Treaty of Versailles but also of the Locarno Pact; Hitler and Mussolini actively intervened in the civil war in Spain, and Germany signed the Anti-Comintern Pact with Japan. Then, in 1937, Japan launched her all-out invasion of China.

Because of its preoccupation with the domestic crisis, the Roosevelt administration was unable to react decisively to these increasing signs of international disorder. Strengthened by revelations of alleged complicity of bankers and munitions makers in America's entry into the First World War, the isolationist movement retained great popularity, and Congress passed a series of neutrality acts designed to keep the country out of war. In a speech at Soldiers Field in Chicago in 1937, the President might call for a "quarantine" of aggressors, but he was unable to modify the prevailing pacifist mood. This situation was not materially affected by Hitler's seizure of Austria in March 1938: nor did it change in response to the Sudeten crisis later that year, nor when at Munich the Western powers in effect signed away Czechoslovakia's future. So strong were the isolationists that in January 1938 a proposed constitutional amendment requiring a plebiscite prior to a declaration of war was barely defeated. To be sure, stunned by the savagery of the anti-Semitic excesses during the so-called "Night of Crystal," Roosevelt withdrew the American Ambassador from Berlin, but neither Germany's seizure of the remainder of Czechoslovakia the following March nor Hitler's sarcastic reply to Roosevelt's request for future guarantees were able to shake the prevailing isolationism of the American people. As late as spring and early summer of 1939, Congress refused to comply with the administration's suggestion to repeal the arms embargo provisions of the Neutrality Act. Roosevelt favored a "cash and carry" clause permitting belligerents to obtain materiel if they paid for it and carried it away in their own bottoms. That this change would have benefited Great Britain and France because of their control of the seas, however, made no difference. In fact, Senator William E. Borah, the powerful isolationist member of the Foreign Relations Committee, in reply to the State Department's warning that war might shortly break out in Europe, insisted that according to his private sources this information was untrue.

Then, in August, Hitler and Stalin concluded their non-aggression pact. Freed from the fear of a two-front war, Hitler served an ultimatum on Poland in which he demanded the return of Danzig and the cession of a road through the Polish Corridor. When he met with a refusal, he launched his attack on September 1. Great Britain and France, loyal to their treaty obligations, then declared war on Germany. World War II in Europe had begun.

American Aid to the Allies Short of War. The outbreak of war in Europe made it necessary for the United States to take some sort of action. The defeat of Great Britain and France, two fellow democracies, would so upset the balance of power in the Old World that American interests, if not American security, would be severely endangered. The triumph of totalitarianism at the expense of the leading democratic countries would imperil the survival of free government everywhere; the victory of an autocratic economic system in Europe would encourage similar experiments in other parts of the world and constitute a grave threat to the American economy.

Roosevelt and his advisers were fully aware of these problems; the persistence of isolationism in the United States, however, created difficulties. In view of the strength of the antiwar movement, it would not be easy to extend support to the Allies. Every effort to help them would be branded as a deliberate step toward war, and, although the majority of the American people favored Great Britain and France, that same majority was firmly opposed to active American participation in the conflict.

As long as it seemed feasible to help the Western powers with measures short of war, it might be possible to obtain the appropriate legislation. But once this was no longer enough, there would be real trouble.

In 1939, at the time of the outbreak of hostilities, both the administration and the public seem to have been convinced that the Allies would be able to prevail without direct American participation. To make sure that they would obtain all the help they needed, the President and his supporters introduced legislation for the repeal of the arms embargo. Coupled with rigid cash and carry provisions, the measure passed Congress in November of 1939. By that time, Hitler had already conquered Poland; he might easily have considered the change of the law an unneutral act, but he did not react. Determined to keep the United States as neutral as possible for as long as possible, he refused to be provoked prematurely. In his mind, the reckoning with the hated trans-Atlantic democracy would come later.

In the spring of 1940, Hitler, after conquering Denmark and Norway, succeeded in overrunning Luxembourg, Belgium, Holland, and northern France in quick order. Italy entered the war on Germany's side, and France was forced to conclude an armistice which left the northern and western part of the country under German occupation, while a pro-Fascist government was installed at Vichy. Britain was left to carry on the war alone. Winston Churchill, who now became Prime Minister, thrilled the world with his oratory and leadership in the ensuing Battle of Britain. Whether his beleaguered country would be able to hold out, however, was doubtful.

In this crisis, Roosevelt acted with determination. Vigorously condemning Italy's intervention in a speech at the University of Virginia, he said, "the hand that held the dagger has struck it into the back of its neighbor." He reorganized his Cabinet by including the Republicans Henry L. Stimson and Frank Knox as Secretaries of War and of the Navy. In the course of a vigorous program of rearmament, he finally induced Congress to introduce the country's first peacetime draft. To succor beleagured Britain, he found authority to transfer to the British fifty overage destroyers in return for British bases in the New World. Although this action doubtless stretched traditional views of neutrality, Hitler again did not respond very firmly. To be sure, he entered into the Tripartite Pact with Japan, a treaty which pledged the signatories, Germany, Italy, and Japan, to come to each others' aid if attacked by a power not yet engaged in the war *(see Document No. 1)*; yet he still managed to restrain his hatred for America. Contemplating war against the United States at a later date, he kept his military advisors busy with preparations for the seizure of the Azores and Canary Islands for the purpose. But he wanted to defeat Great Britain first.

This German determination to proceed step by step was not even disturbed by ever more active American aid to Great Britain the following year. After Roosevelt's reelection to an unprecedented third term in November of 1940, it became apparent that Great Britain could no longer afford to pay for needed weapons and ammunition. The answer to this problem was the Lend-Lease Act, H.R. 1776. Empowering the President to lend or lease goods to powers the defense of which he deemed essential for American security, the law was passed in March 1941, after a bitter fight with isolationists in and out of Congress. The administration implemented it by entering into agreements with Denmark for the administration of Greenland (April 1941) and with Iceland for the occupation of that country (July 1941). In this manner, American ships could convoy goods almost to the doorstep of Europe and carry vital materiel a long way toward beleaguered Britain. The German navy, stung by ever increasing aid to the British, demanded the right to fire upon American ships, but Hitler refused. He was still anxious to postpone the showdown with the United States.

Hitler's attack on the Soviet Union on June 22, 1941, created additional problems for Roosevelt. Anti-communism was so strong in America that it was difficult to persuade the public of the necessity of aid for the Soviets; nevertheless, by the fall, the President had overcome this obstacle and Russia became eligible for lend-lease. It was natural that the isolationists were more aroused than ever.

During the summer of 1941, Roosevelt moved closer toward direct American participation in the conflict. In August, he met with Winston Churchill at Placentia Bay in Newfoundland, where he joined with the British leader in issuing the Atlantic Charter. In September, after an incident involving the U.S.S. *Greer* and a German submarine, he issued orders to shoot Nazi U-boats on sight, and in the fall, Congress scrapped important portions of the remaining neutrality legislation. The President had led his country as far as he dared. But although it was obvious that Britain could not win without full American participation, the public still resisted the logic of this conclusion.

America and Japan. For the Japanese, the European war presented unusual opportunities. Regarding Great Britain and the United States as the principal obstacles to their plans of expansion, many of the Empire's military leaders hoped to benefit from the Anglo-Saxon powers' preoccupation in Europe. The fall of France and the conquest of the Netherlands orphaned the two countries' extensive colonial holdings in East Asia, while Britain's plight rendered it difficult for her to extend effective aid to China. Moreover, the Fascist ideology held a certain attraction to extremist circles in Japan, so that the Tripartite Pact of September 1940 was not merely a marriage of convenience. When in early 1941 Foreign Minister Yosuke Matsuoka traveled to Europe to strengthen the pact, he merely gave outward expressions to these sentiments. Urged by Hitler and von Ribbentrop to attack Singapore, he gave serious thought to the suggestion; then, returning to Japan by way of Moscow, he concluded a non-aggression pact with the Soviet Union. In spite of these power-political and ideological ties to the Axis and its then presumed partner, however, Japan was still dependent on the United States for iron, steel, oil, and other essential supplies. And because the Roosevelt administration, after denouncing the 1911 commercial treaty with

Japan, had already curtailed the exportation of some of these raw materials, it became necessary for the Japanese to seek some sort of accommodation with the United States. For this reason, the government of Prince Fumimaro Konoye sent Admiral Kichisaburo Nomura to Washington as Ambassador. Arriving in February 1941, he was to negotiate with the State Department to find some solution to the outstanding problems bedeviling Japanese-American relations.

The conversations between Ambassador Nomura and Secretary of State Cordell Hull continued intermittently from March 1941 until December 7. They were initiated through unofficial channels — two Maryknoll missionaries who were in contact with Postmaster General Frank C. Walker — and substantially began with a draft proposal drawn up at the Japanese Embassy in Washington. Coupling a vague explanation of Japan's obligations under the Tripartite Pact with a request that the United States induce Chiang Kai-shek to come to terms with his enemies by forming a coalition with the Tokyo-installed regime of Wang Ching-wei, it is stipulated that the United States cease all aid to the Generalissimo in case of his refusal. In addition, America was to resume normal trade relations with Japan. Vague references to a "joint defense against communistic activities and economic cooperation" turned out to be thinly veiled demands for continued occupation and exploitation of China. *(See Document No. 2.)* Hull countered with the insistence that prior to any agreement, Japan recognize four fundamental principles, "(1) Respect for the territorial integrity and the sovereignty of each and all nations; (2) Support of the principle of non-interference in the internal affairs of other countries; (3) Support of the principle of equality, including equality of commercial opportunity;" and "(4) Nondisturbance of the status quo in the Pacific except . . . by peaceful means." The Japanese proposals with their demands for Imperial domination of China were naturally unacceptable to the United States, which was committed to the maintenance of that country's independence.

The Japanese insisted on their terms. Submitting revised proposals to the Secretary of State on May 12, they again suggested that the two countries jointly seek to restore peace in Europe and that America cease her assistance to Great Britain. This renewed invitation to give up not merely Chinese independence (an indispensable part of the new proposal as well as of the old) but British survival as well naturally found no favor in Washington. In his reply on June 21, Hull in an oral statement summed up the main points of difference between the United States and Japan: the Tripartite Pact and the continued Japanese presence in China. He also criticized those Tokyo officials eager to collaborate with Hitler *(see Document No. 3)* and handed Nomura a revised American version of the Japanese draft proposals. Matsuoka took great offense at the Secretary's allusion to his activities, and Hull eventually withdrew it. The next day, however, Matsuoka had other matters to think about. Germany attacked the Soviet Union, an event he had failed to foresee.

In the following weeks, despite Matsuoka's desire for close cooperation with the Nazis, the Japanese decided not to break with Russia temporarily pending developments on the Eastern front but to turn south for further conquests, a program made official during a conference "in the Imperial presence" on July 2. *(See Document No. 4.)* Reorganizing his government in such a way as to drop Matsuoka as Foreign Minister, Prince Konoye sought to solve the Empire's difficulties by further negotiations with the United States. From the very beginning, however, it was clear that should these fail to produce the desired results, Japan would resort to war.

The negotiations assumed greater urgency on July 26, when President Roosevelt, following Japan's invasion of southern Indochina, froze all Japanese funds in the United States. This action in effect ended all oil exports to the island empire. Unable to procure the necessary fuel, the Japanese war machine would either have to come to a halt or conquer the Dutch East Indies.

It was precisely to forestall this possiblity, or at least to delay it as long as possible, that Roosevelt and Churchill at their Atlantic Conference decided to send a warning to Japan. Upon his return from Newfoundland, Roosevelt met with Nomura. Should Japan continue her southward expansion, the President told the Ambassador, the United States would have to take the necessary countermeasures.

These developments greatly disturbed Prince Konoye. Pressed on the one hand by the army to go to war with the Western powers and aware on the other of the diffi- culties of a conflict with the United States, the Prime Minister sought a way out in a personal meeting with President Roosevelt. In the quiet atmosphere of Hawaii, he thought, perhaps he might reach an understanding with the President. But Roosevelt and Hull, uncertain of the Prince's real power and intentions, demanded some prior agreement on principles. This the Prime Minister was unable to give. In the course of an Imperial confer- ence on September 6 (see Document No. 5), the military and Konoye agreed to go to war should the negotiations with America fail. Unable to give his assent to prior con- ditions acceptable to the army, the Prime Minister could not carry out his plans for the summit conference. The military leaders became more insistent than ever, and on October 16, after first attempting in vain to obtain the cooperation of the navy, the Prince tendered his resigna- tion. His successor was General Hideki Tojo, the Minister of War, who was pledged to carry out the army's bidding. (See Document No. 6.)

Although Tojo was perfectly willing to resort to war, even he was not ready to abandon diplomacy altogether. In a conflict with the Western powers, eventual success was uncertain, especially as Hitler had not defeated Russia as quickly as expected. Under these circumstances, Tojo sent the career diplomat Saburo Kurusu to Washington to assist Nomura. But he warned the two ambassadors. Negotiations must be completed by November 25, a dead- line he later changed to the 29th.

The cryptic references to a rigid time limit were the only indications to the Japanese ambassadors of their country's war plans. Totally unknown to them and to the majority of their compatriots, supersecret plans had been devised by Admiral Isoroku Yamamoto, the commander of the combined Japanese fleet, to attack American Naval units at Pearl Harbor. Japanese carriers protected by auxiliary vessels would secretly steam out of Hitokappu Bay in the Kuriles, sail across the little frequented Northern Pacific Ocean under complete radio silence, and then, within about 250 miles of Hawaii, release their plans for an attack on the unsuspecting American fleet. The very latest time at which this plan could be carried out with any hope of success was the beginning of December; thereafter weather conditions would render it impracticable until the following spring. By that time, however, Japan would be very short of oil. Yamamoto's planning was meticulous. But its success depended on complete surprise.

Nomura was now given two proposals to present to the Americans. The first, Proposal "A," suggested resumption of normal trade, the withdrawal of Japanese troops from China "after a suitable interval" (Tokyo was thinking of twenty-five years) following the conclusion of peace between China and Japan, and the end of Japanese occupation of French Indochina. Should this be rejected by the United States, the Tojo government had prepared another proposal, "B," a sort of *modus vivendi,* which obligated the United States not to hinder peace negotiations with China and provided for the resumption of normal trade relations. *(See Documents No. 7 and 8).* Under pressure from his military and naval advisers to gain time, Roosevelt at first believed that some sort of temporary agreement might indeed be reached, and between November 22 and 25, the State Department prepared a *modus vivendi* of its own. This would have pledged both countries not to advance by force into any area in East Asia or the Pacific, asked Japan to withdraw from southern Indochina while reducing her forces in the north, and modified mutual freezing orders to permit, among other things, the shipment of oil for civilian needs. The United States would use its good offices to obtain similar agreements from Britain, Australia, and the Netherlands, and would expect peace talks between China and Japan to be based upon "fundamental principles of peace, law, order and justice." *(See Document No. 9)*.

Nothing came of this proposed patching up of outstanding issues, however. Fears in Great Britain and especially in China, as well as the news of a Japanese naval convoy moving into the South China Sea, caused the Roosevelt administration to give up plans for an accommodation with Japan. Instead, on November 26, Secretary Hull handed the two ambassadors a ten-point note restating the fundamental American position. Demanding that Japan withdraw completely from China and Indochina, it promised in return that the United States would restore normal trade relations to help solve Japanese economic problems. In addition, it required the Imperial government for all practical purposes to nullify the Tripartite Pact. *(See Document No. 10.)*

The Pearl Harbor Attack. It was clear to the administration that Japan's acceptance of this plan was most unlikely. Consequently, General Marshall and Admiral Stark sent war warnings to the commanders of the United States installations in the Pacific. But the President was not sure of the next step. Believing that a Japanese attack would take place in Southeast Asia, in Thailand, Malaya, or the East Indies, he did not know what action the United States could take.

Contrary to expectations, nothing overt happened on Saturday, November 29, or on Sunday, November 30, the first weekend following the delivery of the ten-point note. Unknown to the United States, however, in accordance with decisions taken on November 5, war was finally determined upon in an Imperial conference on December 1. Then, on December 6, the Japanese reply to the American proposal began to arrive. It was so long that it was not completely intercepted until the next morning, but its tenor was such that it seemed to indicate the certainty of war with the United States. When on December 7 Nomura and Kurusu received instructions to deliver the note to the Secretary of State at 1:00 p.m., Washington time, it became evident that time was running out. After some delay, General Marshall sent an additional warning to the commanders in the field, only to run into technical difficulties in its transmittal to Hawaii. Thus it failed to arrive in time, and at 1:50 p.m. Washington learned that Pearl Harbor had been attacked. War had come to the United States.

CHAPTER TWO

THE CONTROVERSY ABOUT FRANKLIN D. ROOSEVELT

Because the Pearl Harbor attack, by unifying the country in support of the war effort, solved Roosevelt's principal foreign policy problem, it is not surprising that his role in the disaster has become most controversial. For years isolationist writers had accused him of trying to drag the country into a foreign war. Some, like George Morgenstern, certain that the New Deal had not succeeded in restoring the American economy, believed that the President was trying to solve his domestic problems by the age-old method of looking for foreign adventures. Others were less specific, but the more Roosevelt emerged as a great wartime leader the more they became convinced that he had sought such a role all along. *Back Door to War,* Charles C. Tansill called his study of the President's diplomacy prior to World War II. Emphasizing Roosevelt's alleged failure to goad Hitler into a declaration of war, Tansill charged that the President then provoked the Pacific conflict as another method to achieve the same end. As time went on, the accusations became ever more extreme. Millions of Americans became convinced that while their President was ostensibly busy with his stamp collection in the White House, he was actually awaiting news of the expected attack on Pearl Harbor, which he himself had provoked by deliberately baiting the Japanese with the fleet he himself had stationed at Hawaii. Secretary of Labor Frances Perkins's recollection of his allegedly relaxed attitude after the event seemed to give added impetus to this theory of conspiracy.

On the face of it, this hypothesis is most improbable and inconsistent. As Thomas A. Bailey and Paul B. Ryan have pointed out, no sane leader, much less a lover of ships like Roosevelt, would deliberately risk his fleet to serve as bait. Because of this theory's persistence, however, it is necessary to examine it more closely.

Placing the Fleet at Pearl Harbor. The normal anchorage of the United States fleet in the Pacific was at San Diego and San Pedro, California. When in the spring of 1940 in the course of maneuvers it arrived at Pearl Harbor, the President, anxious to deter Japanese aggression in the Dutch East Indies, ordered that it be kept there. Admiral James O. Richardson, its commander, objected. Considering Pearl Harbor a poor anchorage, he believed that far from deterring the Japanese, the fleet placed there in its then state of unpreparedness would have the opposite effect. He favored its return to the West Coast for immediate correction of its evident shortcomings in preparation and morale. This was the point of view he represented when in October he came to Washington. Handing a memorandum containing his ideas to the Secretary of the Navy and the Chief of Naval Operations, he made his opposition known. In addition, he forcefully expressed his opinions at a luncheon with the President. The presence of the fleet in Hawaii might influence a civilian government, he said, but Japan had a military government to which it was no secret that the fleet was undermanned, unprepared for war, and, lacking a train of auxiliary ships, unable to undertake offensive operations. Thus it could not exercise a restraining influence on the Japanese and it would be advisable to return it to California. There its complements could be filled, the ships fully supplied with ammunition, provision, stores, and fuel, and then stripped for active operations. According to the Admiral, this course of action was much more likely to impress the Japanese. But Roosevelt was not convinced. "Despite what you believe," he said, "I know that the presence of the fleet in the Hawaiian area, has had, and is now having, a restraining influence on the actions of Japan." The Admiral disagreed, and further conversation revealed that the President was certain of the likelihood of war, either sooner or later. While Admiral William D. Leahy, who was also present, failed to corroborate these details, he confirmed Richardson's insistence that the fleet was ill-prepared.

While he was in Washington, Richardson also learned
that the President was worried about Japan's reaction to
Britain's imminent reopening of the Burma Road, the
main supply line to China. Roosevelt, said the Secretary
of the Navy, was prepared to respond forcefully to any
drastic Japanese moves. To shut off trade between the
island empire and the Americas, he was thinking of estab-
lishing a Naval patrol of light ships in two lines from
Hawaii to the Philippines and from Samoa to the Dutch
East Indies. Richardson objected. The plan would surely
lead to war, he said, and the Navy was not prepared for
conflict. He heard nothing more about the projected
patrol.

On February 1, 1941, Richardson was relieved of
command and replaced by Admiral Kimmel. When he returned to Washington, he asked the Secretary of the
Navy why his tour of duty had been cut short. "The
last time you were here you hurt the President's feel-
ings," was the reply. Later magnified by revisionist
writers, this contretemps contributed to the rumors of
Roosevelt's alleged high-handed treatment of the Navy.

Grew's Warning. On January 27, 1941, Joseph C.
Grew, the American Ambassador to Japan, one of the
President's intimates, made the following entry in his
diary: "There is a lot of talk around town to the effect
that the Japanese, in case of a break with the United
States, are planning to go all out in a surprise mass attack
on Pearl Harbor." He had heard specific rumors to that
effect from his Peruvian colleague and so informed the
State Department. As time went on, however, neither
the Ambassador nor his superiors gave much weight to
these unsubstantiated reports. But if Grew discounted
this specific information, he was under no illusions about
Japan's general mood and capabilities. On November 3,
he cabled to Washington that it would be very short-
sighted to base American policy on the belief Japanese
preparations for war were mere saber rattling. "Japan's
resort to measures which might make war with the United
States inevitable may come with dramatic and dangerous
suddenness," he added. Of course he had no idea that by

that time the Japanese high command had actually decided upon an attack on Pearl Harbor. But his warnings provided ammunition for the President's critics.

The Joint Staff Conversations. After President Roosevelt's reelection in November 1940, American military and Naval leaders entered into secret staff conversations with their British counterparts. These talks, contrary to assertions of their binding nature, were designed to formulate contingency plans for American collaboration with the Allies "should the United States be compelled to resort to war." Taking place in Washington between January 29 and March 27, 1941, they resulted in a report labeled ABC-1, upon which Rainbow 5, the American Naval war plan for operations in the Pacific, also called WP Pac-46, was based. Although the report was initialed by the Secretary of War and the Secretary of the Navy, on June 7, the President returned it without approval. Thus it was not binding. It did not require the United States to go to war under certain circumstances, and it was not a secret device whereby the President could commit the country to a foreign conflict without congressional authority.

Economic Pressure on Japan. Starting in July 1939 with the notification of its intention of abrogating the 1911 commercial treaty with Japan, the United States gradually increased economic pressure on the island empire. The treaty expired in January 1940, and to the Japanese Ambassador's request for a renewal, the administration replied that nothing could be done until Japan changed her policy toward China. Although the United States did not at first impose new duties upon Japanese goods, it had given explicit notice of its intention to use economic weapons to keep Japan from overrunning East Asia. In December 1939, the administration imposed a "moral embargo" on the export of high octane aviation fuel; in June 1940, Congress passed the National Defense Act authorizing the President to restrict or prohibit the exportation of strategic materials, and thereafter this provision was used to prohibit the sale of certain raw materials and machine tools, including iron and steel scrap, to Japan. Gradually extending the list, the United States tightened the noose. Thus in June 1941, it required licenses for all oil exports and the prohibition of oil shipments from the Atlantic seaboard except to the Western Hemisphere and to Great Britain. This ruling was merely the prelude to the final interdiction of oil for Japan and the July 26 freezing order for Japanese funds in the United States. According to the revisionists, these measures especially were a clear case of provoking Japan and forcing her to go to war.

In spite of this assertion, it is obvious that the freezing order was merely the culmination of a longstanding policy of attempting to stop Japan by economic means. In the words of Robert J.C. Butow, it was "an appropriate response not only to the Japanese occupation of southern French Indo-China but to the entire trend of Japan's activity on the international scene." In fact, Roosevelt had for some time been restraining his more bellicose advisers. Far from seeking to provoke the Japanese, he had attempted to keep the situation from getting out of control. Secretary of the Treasury Henry Morgenthau, Secretary of War Stimson, and Secretary of the Interior Harold L. Ickes especially were unhappy about the President's hesitation, and it was not until the Japanese had made it clear that they were determined to continue their southward thrust that Roosevelt finally invoked the drastic freezing order. From then on, its possible revocation became one of the most insistent Japanese demands.

Initiation of the American-Japanese Conversations. The conversations which took place in Washington from March until December 1941 between Secretary of State Hull and Ambassador Nomura, later assisted by Saburo Kurusu, have often been cited as an example of President Roosevelt's unwillingness to come to terms with Japan. It has been charged that the administration failed to meet even halfway evident Japanese attempts to reach an understanding, that it did not properly support the efforts of moderates to counter the designs of militants in Tokyo, and that in the end it allegedly goaded Japan into war.

A brief look at the circumstances will serve to clarify this problem. The chief Japanese negotiator, Admiral Nomura, was somewhat deaf and had an imperfect command of English. Consequently, when, following suggestions of Bishop James E. Walsh and Father James M. Drought, Secretary Hull agreed to initiate negotiations on the provisional basis of the draft memorandum prepared by Colonel Hideo Iwakuro, Tadeo Ikawa, and Father Drought, supplemented by the four points the Secretary had submitted to the Ambassador, Nomura did not clearly state to his government the circumstances of its inception. The authorities in Tokyo were confused and believed the draft understanding to have been prepared by the Americans, a misunderstanding which made further progress in the negotiations even more difficult than they already were. In spite of the intransigence of the Japanese, however — they continued to insist on the retention of troops in China and their own interpretation of the Tripartite Pact — Roosevelt and Hull continued with the talks.

Thus, the accusations of the revisionists are difficult to sustain. To be sure, Roosevelt was less than sympathetic to the Japanese government and its expansionist goals, but then Tokyo had for years pursued a policy of imperialism seriously undermining America's position in the Far East. It is often said that this policy was no different from that carried out earlier by Great Britain, the Netherlands, France, and the United States, all of which had long benefited from their own possessions in East Asia; yet the very fact that these powers had established their influence at a much earlier time gave them a stake in the existing status quo, while Japan was trying to upset it by force of arms. Moreover, the United States had already passed legislation to grant independence to the Philippines in 1946. The Japanese, on the other hand, were determined to extend their influence in China and elsewhere. In addition, the Tripartite Pact bound the Empire to the European dictatorships, and although it was defensive in nature, the Axis tie was a great obstacle to the improvement of Japanese-American relations. Committed to the defeat of Hitlerism, the United States had been moving toward ever more active participation in the European war. Could not the Lend-Lease Act, the Shoot-on-Sight Orders, and similar measures be considered as aggressive acts within the meaning of the treaty? Moreover, as Peter Herde has stressed repeatedly, Roosevelt and Hull were convinced of the existence of a world-wide Axis conspiracy of conquest. No substantiation for such a theory has ever been found, but American actions were nevertheless based on the assumption that it was true. In view of Hitler's ever more aggressive behavior, his policy of brutal terror and murder, and the undeniable fact of seeming Japanese parallels, it is hardly surprising that the hypothesis was taken seriously.

Yet Roosevelt's belief in the existence of a joint German-Japanese scheme for conquest did not necessarily mean that he deliberately sought war with the island empire. On the contrary, not only did he attempt to use economic measures to bring Japan to terms, but on the advice of his military aides, he tried to gain as much time as possible and kept negotiating even though the prospects of success were dubious.

Atlantic Conference. The case against the President usually includes his alleged commitments to come to Britain's aid, an engagement he is supposed to have made at the conference off Newfoundland in which he joined with Churchill in issuing the Atlantic Charter. It is true that the British Prime Minister was anxious to obtain guarantees that the United States would resist Japan's expected advance into Southeast Asia; it is also true that he asked the President to give to Nomura a specific warning to that effect. The proposed draft of the notification which the President was to convey to the Japanese read: "Any further encroachment by Japan in the South West Pacific would produce a situation in which the U.S. Government would be compelled to take countermeasures even though these might lead to war between the U.S. and Japan." But upon his return, he was much more cautious. When he saw the Ambassador on August 17, Roosevelt merely told him that if the Japanese government took any further steps in pursuance of a policy or program of military domination by force or threat of force of neighboring countries, the government of the United States would be "compelled to take immediately any and all steps which it may deem necessary toward safeguarding the legitimate rights and interests of the United States . . . ." Whatever Churchill may have thought, the President's commitments remained very vague.

These general facts are easy to ascertain. Yet revisionists like Charles A. Beard, convinced that the conference resulted in secret understandings, have generally quoted Churchill's address to the House of Commons on January 27, 1942, after the attack on Pearl Harbor. "The probability, since the Atlantic Conference . . . that the United States, even if not herself attacked, would come into a war in the Far East," he said, "and thus make final victory sure, seemed to allay some of these anxieties." The Prime Minister's words speak for themselves; that the United States would enter the war in the Pacific, should one break out, was likely, but it was by no means certain. No binding commitment existed.

The Projected Roosevelt-Konoye Meeting. One of the most disputed incidents during the period of Japanese-American negotiations in 1941 was the failure of the projected meeting between President Roosevelt and Prime Minister Konoye, according to Bruce Bartlett, "perhaps the last hope of heading off war." Genuinely anxious for a speedy settlement, albeit on Japan's terms, in August 1941, Prince Konoye conceived of the idea of meeting with the President in Hawaii and concluding an agreement with him. Promising the army and the navy that he would insist on "the firm establishment of the Great East Asia Co-Prosperity Sphere," he obtained their agreement to his plan. His proposals to the President could not differ very much from the original Japanese suggestions; the army would never have countenanced any substantial concessions. In fact, in a secret conversation between

Foreign Minister Teijiro Toyoda and Ambassador Joseph C. Grew on August 18, the Foreign Minister merely said that Japan would not necessarily be bound by her previous reply to American proposals. This response, dated August 6, had promised the evacuation of Indochina upon the conclusion of peace with China, the neutralization of the Philippines, the restoration of normal trade relations, and America's good offices to induce China to negotiate. By September 3, this offer was clarified. It now included a promise that Japan would not advance further than Indochina, that she would interpret the Tripartite Pact independently, and that she would withdraw her troops from China if a treaty could be worked out (without specifying the time limit for the withdrawal). For its part, the United States would drop its trade restrictions. Though agreeing to Hull's four principles, in effect Japan demanded that America abandon China without offering anything tangible in return.

In spite of these drawbacks, Ambassador Grew believed that Konoye was sincere in his efforts to adjust relations. In a personal letter to the President, whom he addressed as "Dear Frank," he stressed his conviction that the Prime Minister's proposals offered a good chance of carrying out a policy opposed by the extremists. "The alternative to reaching a settlement now would be the greatly increased probability of war," he wrote. He did not know, however, that during the Imperial Conference of September 6, the Japanese government had decided to go to war with the United States and Great Britain by late fall unless Japan's demands were met. *(See Document No. 5.)* These demands clearly included a recognition of Japanese dominance in China, the closing of the Burma Road, the freezing of Western military strength in the Far East at its current level, and the restoration of normal trade relations. Even the continued stress on diplomatic efforts was largely due to the intervention of the Emperor, who, on the day preceding the conference, told the chiefs of staff that he was distressed at their emphasis on war rather than diplomacy. After asking Army Chief of Staff

Hajimo Sugiyama how long he thought a war with America would take, he was told that operations in the South Pacific could be disposed of within three months. He reminded Sugiyama that at the time of the outbreak of the "China Incident," when the Chief of Staff had been Minister of War, Sugiyama had said it would be over within a month, and now, after four long years, the incident was not yet concluded. The Chief of Staff tried to excuse himself by pointing out that the extensive hinterland of China had prevented the conclusion of operation according to plan. Hirohito now raised his voice. If the Chinese hinterland was extensive, he said, the Pacific was boundless. During the conference itself, contrary to his traditional silence, he again spoke in favor of diplomacy and read a poem on human brotherhood written by his grandfather, the Emperor Meiji.

But diplomacy or not, there was very little that Konoye could offer to the Americans as long as the army insisted on some fruits of its four-year adventure in China. Should he agree to a peace with Chiang Kai-shek which did not leave the army in control, it was doubtful that he would ever be able to implement it. To be sure, Professors Herde and David Lu, by no means revisionists, have insisted that a summit conference would have been in America's interest. At the very least, it might have led to a breathing spell, perhaps long enough to make it impossible for the Japanese navy to implement its intended strike. Thus Roosevelt and Hull have been criticized for their rigidity. In view of the questionable nature of Konoye's promises and powers, however, it was neither surprising nor foolhardy to insist on prior understandings. The risks of breaking the common front with China, Great Britain, and her allies were too great.

Konoye's Fall. The failure of Konoye's proposal for a personal meeting with the President led directly to his resignation as Prime Minister and his replacement by the Minister of War, Hideki Tojo. *(See Document No. 6.)* In view of the latter's militarist and expansionist views and his long career as spokesman for the military extremists, it might have been assumed in Washington that all hope for a peaceful settlement was gone. Yet, according to Harry Elmer Barnes, one of the leading revisionists, even the new Tojo regime still offered the United States terms that would have protected its legitimate interests. The trouble with these terms, however, as Tojo's biographer, Professor Butow, has repeatedly emphasized, was that under no circumstances did they include any provisions for an unconditional Japanese withdrawal from China. The Japanese army was still insistent on retaining rewards for its long adventure on the mainland, and these included a peace settlement which would have merged the Nationalist government of Chiang Kai-shek with that of the Japanese puppet Wang Ching-wei as well as the retention for an unforeseeable period of time of Imperial forces in designated areas in China. Because American policy was dedicated to the restoration of the complete independence of China — an aim which in itself has been questioned — these terms were not at all acceptable to the United States. If Tojo was not as extreme as has been assumed, his biographer has pointed out that he was fully prepared to assume the leadership of the nation in war should that become necessary. And according to Japan's free choice, war would become "necessary" if the United States failed to yield to the Empire's demands.

The Projected Modus Vivendi. The Tojo government's last efforts were embodied in the two proposals, "A" and "B," which Ambassador Nomura, after November 15, assisted by Saburo Kurusu, presented to Secretary Hull. *(See Documents No. 7 and 8.)* Available previously in the United States because of the *Magic* intercepts, these proposals were known to be Japan's final offer. Because the Army and the Navy had both requested the administration to seek to gain time, some kind of temporary adjustment was for a short while considered seriously in Washington, so that the State Department countered with its own *modus vivendi,* designed to postpone a showdown for at least three months. *(See Document No. 9.)* The

ultimate rejection of these propositions and the abondonment of America's counteroffer have been described by
revisionist authors as the final steps leading to war. "These
proposals adequately safeguarded all American interests
in the Far East and would at least have provided a basis
for further negotiation," Bruce Bartlett has asserted, and
even William L. Langer and S. Everett Gleason, in their
sympathetic treatment of the administration's foreign
policy, have called the abandonment of the *modus vivendi*
a mystery.

In point of fact, however, whatever the exact sequence
of the dropping of the scheme in Washington, it never
had much of a chance of success. Neither the Japanese
Plan "B" — Tojo's *modus vivendi* — nor Secretary Hull's
counterpart held an answer to the problem of Japan's
presence in China. And unless the United States agreed to
the continued occupation of certain parts of that country,
the Japanese government was unwilling to call off its plan
to go to war by the first week of December. According to
Samuel Eliot Morison, such a proposition was appropriate
"for a nation defeated in war," and Hull correctly rejected
it.

To clarify this controversy, the chronology of the
negotiations must be briefly reconsidered. Proposals "A"
and "B" were transmitted to the Japanese embassy in
Washington on November 4, and on the next day, both
General Marshall and Admiral Stark proposed to the President that some sort of *modus vivendi* with Japan be negotiated. Roosevelt thereupon began to press for a truce
of several months duration, although on November 7, at a
meeting of the so-called War Cabinet to consider the
two proposals intercepted by *Magic,* his advisers were
unanimous in their opinion that public sentiment would
back action against Japan should that country attack
British or Dutch territories vital to American security.
On November 20, Nomura and Kurusu handed to the
Secretary of State the Japanese *modus vivendi* and soon
the State Department began the preparation of its own
version. As the Secretary of War confided to his diary,

however, there was little chance that the Japanese would accept it. "In return for their ceasing all aggressive action we were merely to give them enough raw materials to satisfy their civilian population," he wrote. In discussing the situation with the President on November 25, the War Cabinet heard Roosevelt express the opinion, again based on *Magic* intercepts, that "we were likely to be attacked perhaps (as soon as) next Monday, for the Japanese are notorious for making an attack without warning." As Stimson commented, "the question was what we should do. The question was how we should maneuver them into the position of firing the first shot without allowing too much danger to ourselves." *(See Document No. 11.)*

This statement has been endlessly debated and quoted, especially by the revisionists. Beard used it for the title of one of the chapters of his book, *President Roosevelt and the Coming of the War,* and most of his successors have harped on it since. Yet damning as this entry might seem to those convinced of a conspiracy on the part of the President and the Secretary of War, it made perfect sense at the time. Warned by the *Magic* intercepts that the Japanese were about to go to war unless their demands were met in full, Stimson was naturally concerned about the reaction of the public, especially in case the Japanese attacked merely British and Dutch colonial possessions considered vital to America's defense. As Langer and Gleason pointed out long ago, Stimson was anxious to postpone hostilities at least until the military position of the United States in the Far East had been strengthened. Moreover, Leonard Baker has reminded us that "no one seriously considered accepting the Japanese offer. To do so would mean discarding China and perhaps also Russia. No Asian nation could have felt secure before an expanding Japan."

The Ten-Point Note. When on November 26 President Roosevelt and Secretary Hull, in view of the Japanese convoy sailing south from Shanghai and of Chinese and British protests, finally decided to give up their projected *modus vivendi,* and the Secretary of State, anxious to make some sort of reply, submitted his ten-point note *(see Document No. 10)*, it was obvious that the negotiations had in fact broken down. Revisionists have called the note an ultimatum, and few have failed to note Hull's reply to Stimson on November 27, when asked about the *modus vivendi*. "I have washed my hands of it and it is now in the hands of you and Knox — the Army and Navy," he said. Whether or not it was an ultimatum is disputed. Although nothing in the note vaguely resembled the traditional form of one, a final rejection of which leads to a break in relations and often war, John T. Flynn categorically wrote, "This was an ultimatum. Thus FDR obviously chose war." J.B. Crowley, admitting that technically the document was not an ultimatum, nevertheless holds that operationally it meant war. Yet it contained no threats, was not phrased in such a way as to constitute a final offer, and, as Herbert Feis has explained, left Japan with several options. Thus it did not have to lead to hostilities or a diplomatic rupture unless the Japanese chose so to interpret it. Of course, it was clear to the President and his advisers that their antagonists would not accept the proposals, especially as the administration, in Bruce Russett's words, had "raised the ante" by insisting on a withdrawal from all China. This certainly, however, did not necessarily make the note an ultimatum.

Alleged Deliberate Failure to Warn Pearl Harbor. The extreme care with which any information concerning the breaking of foreign codes was safeguarded led to severe restrictions in the dissemination of information based on the *Magic* intercepts. No details about this intelligence were forwarded to General Short and Admiral Kimmel at Pearl Harbor, and the general warnings which were issued seemed, after the event, pitifully inadequate. Consequently it has been charged that the administration deliberately withheld information from the Hawaiian commanders. Although a war warning was sent to both Kimmel and Short on November 27, neither of them was aware that the Japanese had instructions to bring negotiations to a conclusion by November 29, that requests had

gone to Japanese agents to forward details about the disposition of the American fleet at Pearl Harbor, or that
Tokyo had set up a secret code for broadcasts in case
war was imminent. Moreover, there were certain alleged
specific omissions. Admiral Theobald especially has emphasized the fact that early in December, high Naval
authorities refused to send an additional warning prepared
by Commander Arthur H. McCollum, of the Far Eastern
branch of the Office of Naval Intelligence, and that on
the 4th, Colonel Otis K. Sadtler, the chief of the military branch of the Signal Corps, prepared a specific warning about the imminence of war with Japan, which his
superiors were unwilling to transmit. Finally, on December 6, when President Roosevelt received word of the
Japanese answer to the ten-point note, he at first wanted
to call the Chief of Naval Operations. Finding out that
Admiral Stark was at the National Theater watching a
performance of the *Student Prince,* however, he hesi-
tated and refused to have the admiral paged. Moreover,
Roosevelt failed to notify his chief advisers to be on the
alert.

The Three Little Ships. To prove their contention
that, in case the Japanese were planning to move only
against British and Dutch possessions, President Roosevelt was actually trying to provoke an attack against the
United States, revisionists have often cited the incident
of the "three small vessels", or, as Frederick Sanborn has
called it, "the Case of the Cockleshell Warships." "If
Japan was not going to force a war," writes George Morgenstern, "the President was quite willing to do so." The
facts in the matter are briefly as follows. On December 2,
the Chief of Naval Operations informed Admiral Thomas
Hart, the Commander of the Asiatic Fleet at Manila, that
the President directed the charter of three small vessels to
form a "defensive information patrol." To establish their
identity as American men of war, they were to be commanded by a Naval officer, although the employment of
Filipino crews was authorized. Armed with one small gun
and a machine gun, the ships were "to observe and report

by radio Japanese movements in west China Sea and Gulf of Siam." One of these was to be stationed between Hainan and Hue, another off the Indochinese coast between Cam Ranh Bay and Cap St. Jacques, and the third, off Pointe de Ca Mau. The Admiral was to report measures taken as well as other reconnaissance regulary performed at sea and its effectiveness. *(See Document No. 12.)* The three ships were duly prepared, but none of them ever reached its destination. The *Isabel* actually sailed, only to turn back when the Japanese attack occurred; the *Lanikai* had been outfitted and was at the point of departure on December 7, and the third vessel was not yet ready. Although both Admirals Stark and Hart explained that they thought the order was perfectly proper and warranted under the circumstances — the Japanese were sending large naval forces into the South China Sea — to those critical of the President the event constituted a sure indication that Roosevelt was fishing for an incident. "What a smart plan it was," wrote Frederick Sanborn, castigating "the beguiling and misleading name . . . , 'defensive information patrol,' " the use of the American flag and the attempt to convert "these pitifully 'small' chartered vessels into U.S. men-of-war," and the provocation offered by stationing them in the way of the Japanese fleet. The commander of the *Lanikai,* Admiral Kent Tolley, wrote an entire book about his adventures, a work in which the initial chartering of the ship plays a major role because he believed himself to have been used as "bait." Describing the pitifully insufficient armament and equipment of the vessel, he naturally concluded that she was merely a cog in the larger plan to involve the United States and Japan in hostilities. And the latest revisionist work, Bruce Bartlett's *Cover Up,* describes the ships as "inexpensive *casus bellorum,*" set up to provide the minumum excuse for American retaliation.

How significant the order to Admiral Hart was is difficult to determine. On the face of it, it appears as a perfectly straightforward effort to gather additional information about the Japanese fleet which was known to be steaming toward the south. According to Langer and Gleason, whose explanation Roberta Wohlstetter accepts, the patrol was ordered in response to British pressure for cooperation in keeping watch in the South China Sea and the Gulf of Siam. The peculiar circumstances surrounding it, however, especially the fact that the President himself gave the order and that the ships were so insignificant, will probably always continue to raise questions about the incident.

The Merle-Smith Messages and the Creighton Telegram. "How We Entered the War Four Days Before Pearl Harbor," Harry Elmer Barnes entitled a chapter of his last pamphlet, *Pearl Harbor After a Quarter of a Century.* Recounting in some detail the messages passed during the period in question between Washington, London, Melbourne, Singapore, and Manila, he concluded that after December 4, the ABC agreements and Rainbow 5 had already been implemented, so that Roosevelt's decision on the 6th to send a telegram to the Emperor of Japan was merely a blind to establish a good record. Other revisionists have also emphasized the alleged implementation of the agreements, although their assertions are based on purely circumstantial and sometimes hearsay evidence.

The train of events giving rise to this accusation is as follows. On November 30, in a message to the President, Winston Churchill suggested the United States issue a plain declaration that any further act of aggression by Japan would lead to the gravest consequences. He wanted an assurance of American aid in case the Japanese struck at the British Empire in East Asia. On the same day, Lord Halifax, the British Ambassador in Washington, warned Hull that the Japanese were about to attack Thailand and asked what the United States would do if Britain should resist an advance into the Isthmus of Kra. Unable to give a clear-cut answer, the Secretary of State promised to take up the matter with the President when the latter returned from a brief rest at Warm Springs, Georgia. Hull did so, but Roosevelt did not make a firm decision. When on December 5 Halifax saw Hull again and insisted that the time for immediate cooperation with the Dutch in the East Indies had come, the Secretary expressed his "appreciation of this view." Halifax, however, seems to have interpreted the American replies to his entreaties as positive answers, for on December 4 (December 3, Washington time), the American military attaché in Melbourne, Colonel Van S. Merle-Smith, was told by the Australian government that the Netherlands had invoked the Dutch portion of the Joint War Plans. Sending a cable to this effect to the Philippines, Hawaii, and Washington, he complained that the message had been held up for 17 hours by the Australians. *(See Document No. 13.)*

The British really appear to have believed that they could count on American help. On December 6, Washington time, Admiral Hart in Manila received a telegram from Captain John M. Creighton, the American Naval Attaché in Singapore, with the information that Air Chief Marshal Sir Robert Brooke-Popham, the British commander at Singapore, had received new instructions from London. According to this intelligence, the British had assurances of American armed support in case of a Japanese landing in Thailand or if Britain went to the defense of the Netherlands to ward off an attack on the Dutch East Indies. *(See Document No. 14.)* In view of the fact that on December 2, the American Ambassador in London, John G. Winant, had informed the State Department that the British had news about Japanese movements toward the Isthmus of Kra and other places in the South China Sea, and that on December 6, he mentioned Britain's desire to carry out the President's wishes as expressed in the message transmitted by Sumner Welles to Halifax, *(see Document No. 15.)* Roosevelt's critics have concluded that by that time some sort of understanding to come to the European powers' aid should Japan attack their possessions must have been reached. Other authorities, however, especially Professor Robert A. Divine and Ladislas Farago, show that no binding commitments existed. As Langer and Gleason have pointed out, as late as December 6, the President was still undecided about the matter. That afternoon he conferred with the Australian Minister, Richard G. Casey, who informed his government that Roosevelt had determined to send a special message to the Emperor of Japan. If he did not obtain a reply by Monday night, December 8, he would issue an agreed upon warning to the Japanese on Tuesday afternoon or evening, with the British following with a parallel notification the next day. Thus, it appears that prior to the attack on Pearl Harbor, no hard and fast decisions had yet been made in the White House, except that further warnings were to be sent to the Japanese.

Roosevelt's Last Minute Actions. President Roosevelt's actions, or lack of actions, on December 6 and 7, have also been the source of severe criticism. After seeing the Australian Minister on Saturday afternoon, the President spent the evening with his close companion and adviser, Harry Hopkins. At about 9:30 that night, Lieutenant Lester R. Schulz, the communications assistant to the White House Naval aide, Captain John R. Beardall, came in with a locked pouch containing the intercepted thirteen parts of the fourteen-part Japanese answer to the last American proposals. The President was seated at his desk. He read the documents while Hopkins was slowly pacing back and forth. Then Roosevelt gave the papers to his companion, who read them and handed them back to the President. "This means war," exclaimed Roosevelt, and Hopkins agreed. Discussing the location of the Japanese forces, their deployment, and especially their presence in Indochina, the two men wondered where the next strike would fall. In reply to the President's reference to his message to Hirohito about the forces already in Indochina with a request for their withdrawal, Hopkins expressed the view that since war was undoubtedly going to come at the convenience of the Japanese, it was too bad that the United States could not strike the first blow and prevent any sort of surprise. Nodding, the President answered: "No, we can't do that. We are a democracy and a peaceful people." Raising his voice for emphasis, he added: "But we have a good record." It was then that he said he would have to talk to Admiral Stark and failed to do so until later because he was afraid that paging Stark at the theater would cause public alarm. *(See Document No. 16.)*

On the next day, December 7, Roosevelt met with the Chinese Ambassador and prepared for a family luncheon. When he heard of the Pearl Harbor attack, he was utterly surprised. At the Cabinet meeting that evening, Secretary of Labor Frances Perkins noticed that a change had come over him since she had last seen him two days before. "In spite of the horror that war had actually been brought to us," she wrote, "he had, nevertheless, a much calmer air. His terrible moral problem had been resolved by the event." His critics have cited this observation as proof of his scheming all along for an attack and his satisfaction at having succeeded. A simpler explanation would be that it was merely the obvious relief shown by a man who had been worried about the probability of an attack on British and Dutch possessions and the country's unwillingness to go to war in their defense.

Franklin D. Roosevelt's Aims and Purposes. The President's long term aims are crucial for an understanding of the controversy surrounding the Pearl Harbor attack. Charles C. Tansill's "backdoor to war" thesis has already been mentioned. In its most extreme version it is found in Admiral Theobald's book, *The Final Secret of Pearl Harbor,* which charges that the American fleet was purposely left at an insecure mooring in order to induce the Japanese to attack it; the improbability of a naval-minded President deliberately sacrificing his ships at the outbreak of hostilities, however, has made this charge less common in recent years. Such writers as Bartlett and Tolley feel that not the American fleet at Pearl Harbor, but the three small vessels were the means by which Roosevelt sought to goad the Japanese into an incident, even though the President's defenders have stressed his basic character as good evidence to the contrary. "In the end the American people would judge the record that had been made, and the decency they understood to be within Franklin

Roosevelt, against the calumnies hurled at him, and they would know if war came it had not been sought," Leonard Baker asserts in his *Roosevelt and Pearl Harbor*. And if it may be conceded that he was not entirely candid with the public, one of the principal accusations of Beard and his followers, who have never tired of reminding their readers of Roosevelt's 1940 promise not to lead the country into foreign wars, defenders of the President have stressed the prevailing climate of public opinion at the time. Despite the evident horror of Hitlerism, despite the Nazi threat to the security of the United States, the isolationists still commanded a great number of votes in Congress, as well as support in the country. "In this unsteady climate," Gloria J. Barron has concluded, "and with American involvement in the war uppermost in the public mind, the administration could not have afforded complete candor." In fact, the charge against the President of deliberately withholding information from local commanders is not taken seriously by most modern historians. Roosevelt, it is true, realized that for the survival of the United States and the salvation of the democratic form of government it was necessary for the country to become actively involved in the war. Unsure of how to react to a Japanese attack on British and Dutch colonial possessions, he planned to rouse the country to active measures if it occurred. His problem was solved for him by the attack on Pearl Harbor. That he planned it that way is not really plausible.

"*In a forthcoming book by John Toland, *Infamy: Pearl Harbor and Its Aftermath,* the author revives charges of FDR's foreknowledge of the attack. Maintaining that the Twelfth Naval District in San Francisco intercepted signals of Admiral Nagumo's fleet, he accuses the administration of withholding this intelligence in the belief that American defenses were strong enough to deal with it. Japanese sources, however, have consistently emphasized the fact that the fleet sailed under strict radio silence so that no signals could have been intercepted."

CHAPTER THREE

THE CONTROVERSY ABOUT AMERICAN KNOWLEDGE OF JAPANESE INTENTIONS

Central to the Pearl Harbor controversy is the question of how much Washington knew about Japan's intentions. In view of the fact that United States intelligence specialists had long since cracked many Japanese codes, including the so-called *Purple* diplomatic code, the famous *Magic* process, it has often been assumed that it must have been impossible for the American authorities to have been surprised by the Japanese attack. This sort of reasoning naturally tends to strengthen revisionist arguments. It is therefore necessary to examine the extent of America's foreknowledge in more detail.

The Magic Intercepts. Ever since August 1940, the United States had been able to read the Japanese diplomatic code, usually referred to as *Purple.* The cryptologist responsible for this feat was Colonel William F. Friedman, who, however, later suffered a nervous breakdown and played no part in the period immediately preceding Pearl Harbor. Because of the great difficulty of breaking highly complex codes, the fact that American intelligence had cracked *Purple* was a closely guarded secret. Only a few selected top rank officials had access to it lest it be compromised, and by the fall of 1941, the commanders at Pearl Harbor were definitely not among those privileged to receive the information. In addition, any intelligence gained from these intercepts was also treated with great secrecy in order not to tip off potential enemies that their communications were insecure. These extraordinary precautions later caused grave complications; responsible officers, for example, refused to use scrambler telephones for fear they would compromise the secret.

In the conversations between Admiral Nomura and Secretary Hull, the *Magic* intercepts were of great help to the Americans. Generally well informed about his opposite's instructions, Hull could conduct himself accordly. In addition, he often knew what Japan's minimum and maximum concessions were. In fact, so expert were the cryptologists that the Secretary was frequently in possession of Japanese documents before Nomura himself had deciphered them.

A good example of the benefits derived from the intercepts was the prompt knowledge in Washington of the decisions taken at the Imperial Conference in Tokyo on July 2. This meeting, it will be recalled, was crucial in the development of Japan's war plans. Reaffirming their decision to establish a "Greater East Asia Sphere of Co-Prosperity," the conferees agreed that the Empire would do everything possible to dispose of the war in China and take measures to advance toward the south. For the time being, they did not plan any action against Russia. Diplomatic means were to be employed to come to terms with the United States, but should these fail, Japan, reserving to herself the right to decide when force was to be used, would act in accordance with the Tripartite Pact. *(See Document No. 4.)*

The intercepts were also useful in affording insights into the thinking of the Japanese government. The origin, development, and purpose of Prince Konoye's offer to meet with the President, as well as the dangers which faced the Prime Minister at home, were expressed in several intercepts of telegrams he sent to Nomura. On September 3, for example, a cable from Tokyo to the Japanese embassy in Washington stated that because the existence of the Prime Minister's message had become known to the public, the "gang that has been suspecting that unofficial talks were taking place, has really begun to yell and wave the Tripartite banner." On September 27, the Foreign Minister wrote that "in view of internal and external circumstances in our country, we cannot keep postponing matters forever," and on the next day, he wired that the tendency to oppose an adjustment with the United States was increasing. "Hence," he concluded, "now is the time, if ever, to concentrate on this accord." These intercepts, taken together with Ambassador Grew's advice to meet the Japanese Prime Minister, have given rise to charges that the United States deliberately neglected to take advantage of an excellent opportunity to arrive at a last understanding with Japan. Nevertheless, they may also be interpreted as certain signs of the unreliability of the promises of the Japanese government.

Valuable though it was, not even *Magic* could keep the United States informed about every important event in Tokyo. For example, the record of the Imperial Conference of September 6, at which it was definitely decided to go to war with the Western powers unless they agreed to Japan's demands by the end of October *(see Document No. 5)*, was not transmitted in *Purple* code. These demands still envisaged the abondonment of China by the United States, and in view of the decisions already taken it was evident that no agreement not including a complete surrender of the American position had any chance of success. Other matters that remained hidden were the circumstances of Konoye's resignation, Japanese military and naval plans, and the exact relationship between the Japanese army, navy, and government.

The "Bomb Plot" and Ships-in-Harbor Reports. In determining whether Washington had any foreknowledge of the Pearl Harbor attack, the so-called "bomb plot" and ships-in-harbor messages play a crucial role. The messages in question concern directives to Japanese agents in Hawaii. On September 24, the Japanese Foreign Office instructed its operatives at Honolulu henceforth to make meticulous reports regarding the ships at Pearl Harbor. The spies were to divide the base into five subareas, A through E, and to identify warships and aircraft carriers as at anchor, tied up at wharves, buoys, and docks, with special attention to two or more vessels alongside the same wharf. *(See Document No. 17.)* Because it was not sent in *Purple* but in a less secure code (J-19), the intercepted message was not decoded in Washington until October 9.

The main Japanese agent in the Hawaiian Islands was Ensign Takeo Yoshikawa. Working in the Japanese consulate-general under the alias of Tadashi Morimura, he meticulously forwarded the required information. On November 15, his superiors ordered him to render his reports twice weekly, and on November 29, to make them even if there was no movement of ships. Then, on December 2, through the consulate-general, he received another crucial message. Informing him that in view of the situation, the presence in port of warships, airplane carriers, and cruisers was of the utmost importance, Tokyo requested him to report every day. In addition, he was asked to find out whether the warships at Pearl Harbor were provided with antimine nets and whether there were any observation balloons above the base or any indications that they might be sent up. (See Document No. 18.) The ensign carried out all these instructions with promptitude and ingenuity and reported his discoveries to Tokyo. But because of the continued use of a code less secure than *Purple*, the translation of some of these intercepted messages was again delayed, this time until after the Pearl Harbor attack.

In later years, the first of these intercepts was called the "bomb plot." The minority report of the Joint Congressional Committee on the Investigation of the Pearl Harbor Attack concluded that "the probability that the Pacific Fleet would be attacked at Pearl Harbor was clear from the 'bomb plot' available in Washington as early as October 9." Revisionist historians have repeated the charge, and the certainty of the "bomb plot's" pointing to an impending attack on Pearl Harbor became one of the accusations against Roosevelt who allegedly had failed to do anything about it.

The difficulty with the "bomb plot" theory is, however, that it is based on hindsight. At the time the September 24 message was received, it made no real impression on the Naval and military establishment. The Chief of Naval Operations, when asked about it by the Joint Committee, could not even remember it; Rear Admiral Theodore S. Wilkinson, the Director of Naval Intelligence, insisted that similar messages concerning Seattle, Bremerton, Long Beach, San Diego, and Panama were routine. He thought they were all part of Japan's general information system, an indication of the "nicety" of Japanese espionage, as the Japanese had the reputation of being meticulous seekers for every scrap of information of possible intelligence value. Commander McCollum of the Far Eastern Section of Naval Intelligence, while admitting that there were no other messages of such precision, nevertheless believed that they might simply have indicated interest in the facility with which the fleet was prepared to move, while his assistant, Lieutenant Commander Alwin D. Kramer, interpreted them as an attempt to simplify communications. After all, the Japanese were closely monitoring shipping movements everywhere. Thus the "bomb plot" and ships-in-harbor messages constitute a good example of Roberta Wohlstetter's explanation of the failure at Pearl Harbor because of the sheer multiplicity of messages, although Kramer did think the original communication important enough to mark it with an asterisk and distribute it to his superiors on a "gist sheet". But even if anybody had attached any significance to the messages, they were thought to be useless to the Japanese. The intelligence community in Washington believed that in accordance with current war plans, in case of a war warning the whole fleet would be at sea.

Why the information was never forwarded to Pearl Harbor is a more serious question. If anybody should have known about Japanese interest in the anchorage of the Pacific Fleet, it was obviously Admiral Kimmel. Yet he neither received the messages nor any summary of them — a good example of the poor dissemination of intelligence information at the time. In mitigation, it may again be said that too many messages concerning too many installations were being intercepted; it would probably have been very difficult to disseminate these regularly to all commands and still have safeguarded the vital secret of the breaking of the codes. Even the friendly majority of the Congressional Committee, however, while insisting that the messages did not point clearly to Pearl Harbor, concluded that they should have been dealt with more carefully.

The Deadlines. In November 1941, the *Magic* intercepts became more ominous. Starting with a message from
Foreign Minister Shigenori Togo to Nomura on November
2, which stated that the forthcoming offer would be "our
last effort to improve diplomatic relations," a sense of
immediacy became more and more evident. On November
4, Tokyo informed the Ambassador that "both in name
and spirit this counterproposal of ours is indeed the last."
If it did not lead to a quick accord, the talks would "certainly be ruptured." And on November 5, Nomura was
told that the agreement had to be completed by the 25th.
(See Document No. 19.)
      What this deadline referred to, unknown to the Ameri-
cans, was the plan to bomb Pearl Harbor. The fleet was
to sail from Hitokappu Bay by that time, and the navy
insisted that any delay would render military operations
impossible for that season.
      Even if the details of the Empire's offensive plans
were not known in Washington, the urgency of the situation became ever more obvious. On the 11th, telegrams
from Tokyo cautioned that the United States was still not
fully aware of the critical nature of the situation, that the
deadline was definite and could not be changed. Japan insisted that the talks could no longer be considered as preliminary; the United States must simply be induced to
sign an agreement by the 25th. On the 16th, the language
became even more insistent. "The fate of our Empire
hangs by the slender thread of a few days, so please fight
harder than you ever did before," read the instructions to
the envoys. And although on the 22nd, the deadline was
extended for a few days, until the 29th, it was made absolutely clear that there would not be a second postpone-
ment. "This time we mean it," the Foreign Office in
Tokyo wrote, "that the deadline absolutely cannot be
changed. After that things are automatically going to happen." *(See Document No. 20.)* Following the abandonment of the *modus vivendi*, the Japanese Ambassadors
were told that Hull's ten-point note was totally unacceptable and that they were to continue to play for time. *(See
Document No. 21.)* Messages from and to the Japanese

Ambassador in Berlin and from areas under Japanese control confirmed the seriousness of the situation, and it was widely believed that Japan would strike on the weekend of the 29th. Under these circumstances, there has been considerable speculation about the failure of the administration to alert its forces more fully. It is certain that the likelihood of war was clearly understood in Washington.

The Window Code, Hidden Words Code, and Code Destruction Messages. In addition to the deadline messages, there were several other indications that war was imminent. One of the most significant of these was the failure to evaluate in time the so-called window code. On December 3, the Japanese consulate-general informed Tokyo that henceforth a different code would be used, specific signals to indicate battleship and carrier movements. These would be in the form of lights shining at certain times from a house at Lanikai Beach and from the attic of another at Kalama. Simultaneously, certain advertisements would appear in the newspapers. Although not sent in *Purple,* this information was being deciphered the morning of December 6. Mrs. Dorothy Edgers, a research analyst in the Office of Naval Intelligence in Washington, who was fluent in Japanese, recognized its more than usual importance and stayed overtime that Saturday to finish the translation. When she left shortly before 2 p.m., she gave the document either to Lieutenant Commander Kramer or to his assistant. Apparently the translation was still in draft form, and Kramer, distracted by the intercept of the pilot message announcing the imminent arrival of the Japanese answer to the ten-point note, put it aside until the following Monday. This episode has been severely criticized by revisionist writers, especially by Professor Barnes, who has maintained that, because the lights might be seen by submarines or other ships, the code clearly pointed to a naval attack on Hawaii.

A similar incident concerns the hidden words code announced by Tokyo on November 27, an arrangement providing for the identification of messages containing certain code words by the inclusion at the end of the English word, STOP. These code words would indicate whether relations between Japan and certain specifically named countries had either been severed, were not in accordance with expectations, or had deteriorated to the point of war. Only one such message, however, was intercepted prior to the Pearl Harbor attack, a cable on December 7 that relations between Japan and England were not in accordance with expectations.

The Japanese also set up a telephone code, in which the President was referred to as Miss Kimiko and the Secretary of State as Miss Umeko. On November 27, American intelligence intercepted a telephone call between Kurusu and the Chief of the American Department of the Tokyo Foreign Office, Kumaichi Yamamoto. The Ambassador, talking guardedly about a "matrimonial question" and an interview with Miss Kimiko, said a crisis was at hand, only to be told to keep negotiating. As Japan would not yield, the negotiations were evidently a cover for something else. This was especially true because on December 1 the Japanese navy, for the second time within a month, changed all its call signals.

One additional indication should be cited. *Magic* made available to Washington Japanese instructions to overseas personnel to burn papers and destroy code machines. The code destruction message was intercepted on December 2, translated on the third, and evaluated at that time. Colonel Rufus S. Bratton, the Chief of the Far Eastern Section of Army Intelligence, sent an assistant to the Imperial Embassy in Washington to verify the information and found out that the Japanese were actually burning their papers. So important did he deem this message that he took it to Generals Sherman Miles, the Acting Assistant Chief of Staff, G-2, and Leonard T. Gerow, Chief of the Operations Division, to induce them to send further warnings to the commanders in the field. Gerow, however, thought that enough alerts had already been sent out, and because of restrictions on intelligence transmittal of operational material without clearance from the Operations Division, Miles felt that he could not act on his own.

Bratton refused to give up. He conferred with his Naval counterpart, Commander McCollum, whom he told of his concern. McCollum agreed with the Colonel about the importance of the intercept. He also shared with Bratton his own worry about the Winds messages and said that Commander Joseph J. Rochefort, the Naval combat intelligence officer in Hawaii, had all the information needed. Now Bratton, more anxious than ever to warn Pearl Harbor, decided to alert Lieutenant Colonel Kendall J. Fielder, the Hawaiian command's G-2, to get in touch with Rochefort. In this roundabout manner, he hoped to circumvent the difficulty about operational matters. General Miles was willing; the telegram was sent, but Fielder failed to obtain the information.

The Winds Code. One of the most disputed questions about the Pearl Harbor attack is the problem of the receipt prior to the raid of a so-called Winds-Execute message. The Winds code was an arrangement set up by the Japanese in November, regarding the broadcast of a special message in case of an emergency. Under such circumstances, warnings were to be added in the middle and at the end of the daily Japanese language shortwave news broadcasts, each sentence to be repeated twice. "In case of Japanese-U.S. relations in danger," the wording was to be "HIGASHI NO KAZEAME" (East Wind Rain); in case of Japanese-Soviet relations, "KITANO-KAZE KUMORI" (North Wind Cloudy), and in case of Japanese-British relations, "NISHI NO KAZE HARE" (West Wind Clear). The Japanese also provided for the adding of code words to be inserted at the beginning and end of their intelligence broadcasts when diplomatic relations were becoming precarious. "HIGASHI" referred to relations with the United States, "KITA," to those with Russia, and "NISHI," to those with Geat Britain, including Thailand, Malaya, and the Netherlands East Indies. *(See Document No. 22.).* The messages had been intercepted and translated by November 28, and in view

of the importance both the Army and Navy attached
to these code words, monitors kept a close watch for
them.

Whether any of these broadcasts were ever received
prior to Pearl Harbor has become a source of major controversy. Captain (then Commander) Laurence F. Safford,
Chief of the Communications Security Section of the
Office of Naval Communications in Washington, whose
mission in 1941 was to gather intelligence on foreign
nations, particularly Japan, insisted that his section received a Winds-Execute message on December 4. According to Safford, on that day, Lieutenant Commander
Kramer came in with a teletype communication, on which
was noted, penciled in Kramer's hand, the translation,
"War with England (including NEI, etc.) War with the
U.S. Peace with Russia." "This is it," said Kramer, and
Safford immediately sent the message to Rear Admiral
Leigh Noyes, his superior. The Admiral then allegedly
telephoned the substance of the message to the War Department, to those entitled to receive *Magic* in the Navy
Department, and to the White House. Within one hour,
Noyes called back and instructed Safford to prepare a
warning to Guam to burn excess codes and ciphers. Such a
message was in fact sent, although the occasion may have
been the intercept of the Japanese code destruction orders.

When this story first came to light, Kramer seemed to
corroborate it. As time went on, however, his recollection
became more and more indistinct, especially after a luncheon with Admiral Stark in September 1945. He denied
ever having written, "War with the U.S.," because the original code said nothing about war, and finally seemed to
remember that the message applied only to Great Britain.
In addition, he believed that any such communication
must have been intercepted on the fifth rather than the
fourth, and was somewhat hazy about the possibility of
his having confused it with a Winds-Execute in relation to
Great Britain. The other participants, Lieutenant Commander Francis M. Brotherhood and Admirals Noyes,
Wilkerson, and Royal E. Ingersoll, had very vague recollections about the facts surrounding the incident. Noyes

believed that he had held it to be not genuine because the phrase, "peace with Russia," did not appear in the original Winds arrangement which had specified the positive rather than the negative from of an impending break; moreover, the disputed intercept was in Morse code and the original instructions had directed voice broadcasts. Admiral Ingersoll, Stark's assistant, remembered that there was some kind of message. He did not consider it important, however, because on the day before he had already been warned by the code destruction intercept and believed that the local security unit at Hawaii also had it. As for Lieutenant Commander Brotherhood, he categorically denied that any such communication had ever arrived. An entirely different one referring to a war with Russia stuck in his memory, but he thought nothing concerning "East Wind Rain" ever reached his desk.

To add to the mystery, the Navy's counterparts in the Army were also unable to recall the Winds-Execute message clearly. Colonel Otis K. Sadtler of the intelligence branch of the Signal Corps confirmed that some message was intercepted; according to his recollection, he received a telephone call from Admiral Noyes on December 5 to the effect that the Winds message was in. But he also remembered that it specified Great Britain, not the United States. He promptly notified Army intelligence, to be specific, Colonel Bratton, whom he found at the office of the G-2, General Miles. Miles and Bratton then sent Sadtler back to Admiral Noyes to find out exactly what the message had stated, but Sadtler was unable to find Noyes. Moreover, as Bratton and his group were waiting for a warning about Japanese relations with the United States, not Great Britain, they were not particularly impressed. The code destruction intercept had already warned them of the imminence of war, although Bratton, when trying to warn Fielder, had reference to a Winds-Execute as well as to the code destruction message.

As the execute signal, if it was received, would have added little to what was already known, the whole incident would ordinarily be of little significance. As time went on, however, it became a focal point of the revisionist argument.

The reason for this concentration on the Winds episode was Captain Safford's singlemindedness. After
initially sharing the general opinion that Admiral Kimmel
had been negligent, Safford eventually came to the conclusion that the Commander of the Pacific Fleet had been
horribly wronged. Discovering that the alleged Winds-
Execute message had never been forwarded to Hawaii, he
began a lengthy investigation. For one thing, he was unable to find the original file. It turned out that in the
folder containing the intercepts Number 70001, translated
on December 3, 1941, appeared to be missing. Although it
was customary to cancel certain numbers for technical
reasons, Safford became convinced that the file had been
removed to cover all traces of the message. And because
Kramer and others increasingly failed to support him, he
became ever more suspicious. His testimony remained the
same throughout the various investigations; Admiral Kimmel was persuaded of the truth of Safford's charges, and
revisionist authors have continued to cite the Winds
Execute episode in their indictment of the administration.
It is true that in 1978 Bruce Bartlett conceded that perhaps before Pearl Harbor Safford was less convinced of
the authenticity of the message than later — after all, he
made no effort to warn the fleet. Yet, even non-revision-
ists have criticized the handling of the incident, especially
the pressure apparently brought to bear upon Kramer in
the course of the luncheon with Admiral Stark. At any
rate, while the message's existence remains in doubt, it
would not really have made much difference.

Last Minute Warnings. If the various deadline and
code-burning messages were clear indications of the gravity
of the situation, a series of last minute communications
became even more significant in the subsequent controversy. The first of these, intercepted on Saturday, December 6, was the so-called pilot message. It was a directive
from the Japanese Foreign Office to the embassy in Washington concerning the reply to the ten-point note. This
answer, to be sent in English, in fourteen parts, "for the
time being" was to be treated with great secrecy. A special

message concerning the time of presenting this memorandum would follow. "However," it concluded, "I want
you in the meantime to put it in nicely drafted form and
make every preparation to present it to the Americans
just as soon as you receive instructions." *(See Document
No. 23.)* The peculiar nature of the prospective reply, the
injunction of secrecy — a separate message enjoined the
Ambassadors not to use a typist in its preparation — and
the precautions concerning the time of delivery were all
unusual and indicative of serious events to come.

The note itself, at least the first thirteen of its fourteen parts, arrived that same evening. A lengthy restate-
ment of Japan's position and a rejection of most of the
proposals made in the ten-point note, it again referred to
Japan's position in China and her loyalty to the Tripartite
Pact as the principal issues between the two nations.
Accusing the United States of scheming to extend the
war, it complained that on the one hand, America was
seeking to secure its rear by stabilizing the Pacific area,
while on the other, it was aiding Great Britain and preparing to attack Germany and Italy, "two powers that are
striving to establish a new order in Europe." *(See Document No. 23.)* While not yet a clear declaration of war, the
first thirteen parts of the memorandum nevertheless indicated that a crisis had been reached.

How serious this crisis was became apparent the next
morning. During the night, the fourteenth part of the
message was intercepted. It charged that the United
States, in collaboration with Great Britain, was attempting
to obstruct Japan's efforts to create "a New Order in East
Asia" and to preserve Anglo-American interests by keeping China and Japan at war. Thus, it pointed out, Japan's
hopes of adjusting relations with America had finally been
lost. "The Japanese Government regrets to have to notify
hereby the American Government," it concluded, "that in
view of the attitude of the American Government it cannot but consider that it is impossible to reach an agreement through further negotiations." *(See Document No.
23.)*

This memorandum, which has been referred to as a declaration of war, was indeed meant as such. But its language did not so specify, although it left little doubt about Japan's readiness to use means other than diplomacy. That this was indeed Japan's intention became likely that Sunday morning with the arrival of still another message from Tokyo ordering the Ambassadors upon receipt of the fourteenth part to destroy their remaining documents, code and cipher machines. In addition, they were instructed to submit the fourteen-part note to the United States government, "if possible to the Secretary of State," at 1:00 p.m. on the 7th, Washington time. *(See Document No. 23.)*

The Question of Foreknowledge of Pearl Harbor. There is thus very little controversy about the fact that Washington was forewarned of the outbreak of hostilities. The Japanese had given instructions to their embassies to destroy codes and burn papers; they had notified their German allies of the imminence of war; they had made repeated references to deadlines late in November after which events were automatically going to happen, and they had finally set an unusual time, a Sunday afternoon, for the presentation of a note which evidently presaged some dramatic action. But did the Washington authorities know where this action was to take place?

Only the most extreme revisionists have definitely accused the administration of knowing beforehand that Pearl Harbor was to be attacked. Harry Elmer Barnes, citing general awareness that Japan was capable of surprise attacks, has concluded that "no top military or civilian authority in Washington on December 7, 1941, should have been surprised at either the place or time of the Japanese attack on the Pacific Fleet at Pearl Harbor." Fleet maneuvers in 1932 and 1938, he has argued, had been based on such an assumption. He has adduced Grew's statement about the warning received from the Peruvian Ambassador, as well as the "bomb plot" and secret word messages. Charles C. Tansill, who has likewise suggested that Roosevelt had some knowledge of the likelihood of an attack on Pearl Harbor, has quoted an alleged statement by Kramer as he delivered the 1:00 p.m. message to Secretary Knox that it indicated "a surprise attack on Pearl Harbor today." Admiral Theobald, certain that there was a deep-laid plot, has relied on a story in the New York *Daily News* of May 17, 1951, according to which the famous Soviet spy, Richard Sorge, had informed the Kremlin of Japan's intentions as early as October 1941, and Admiral Tolley has cited rumors that long before the event the Pearl Harbor plan was picked up by British agents in China.

Other revisionists have relied on innuendo. Charles A. Beard, conceding that there is no direct evidence that Roosevelt knew about Pearl Harbor, has held that every sound rule of naval strategy should have warned the administration that the Japanese would not dare to move while the American fleet was at Pearl Harbor. Thus, even if it did not have any prior information, the administration was "lacking in the discernment and prudence to be expected of men occupying such responsible posts of trust in the Government of the United States." George Morgenstern, likewise, has argued that the fleet at Pearl Harbor was the only element that could possibly interfere with Japan's program. "These strategic considerations alone," he has written, "were sufficient to have demonstrated to Roosevelt and the high command that war against the United States would be inaugurated by a Japanese surprise attack at Pearl Harbor and no place else." Moreover, he has charged that "Stimson knew not only that war was coming, but he knew it would break out at Pearl Harbor." Did he not order a compilation of the location of American men of war in preparation for a conference with the President on December 7?

Even some revisionists have admitted that these accusations are generally somewhat vague and unsubstantiated. Bruce Bartlett, for example, believes that while Roosevelt expected hostilities to start by December 7, he did not know that war was going to begin at Pearl Harbor. Indeed, the evidence is very clear that although Washington was

aware of the likelihood of war by December 7, it had no
real information about the place at which the outbreak of
a conflict might be expected. The Secretary of War met
with Hull and Knox at 10:00 a.m. that morning. Hull was
sure that the Japanese were planning some "deviltry," but
the three men were wondering where the blow would fall.
And well they might. For while it is true that the various
spy meassages sent out from Hawaii might have alerted
those who intercepted them, details about other locations
were also broadcast. The very volume of the intercepts,
as Roberta Wohlstetter has shown, strongly militated
against correct evaluations on the part of American intelligence. As for Kramer's statements, they are unsubstantiated; in fact, he denied that he had ever made them, although he did mention that 1:00 p. m. in Washington
corresponded to dawn at Pearl Harbor.

Finally, the very nature of Japan's desperate gamble
made it difficult for Americans to predict it. Fully aware
of the fact that the fleet at Pearl Harbor was not strong
enough to interfere materially with any Japanese advances
into the southwest Pacific, American experts found it
hard to assume that the Imperial navy did not have the
same information. As Colonel Bratton put it so cogently:
"It did not appear logical . . . for Japan to go out of her
way deliberately to attack an American installation. As
a matter of fact, I think the attack on Pearl Harbor was
the stupidest thing the Japanese ever did. If they had gone
about their way down through the Netherlands Indies,
Malaya, Indochina, and leave us stewing in our own juices,
the war might still be on, or we might still be arguing here
as to what to do about it. We might never have declared
war on Japan. But by this deliberate attack upon an
American fortress in the Mid-Pacific she inflamed the
American people to such an extent that we had nothing
left to do, we had to go to war." That this was also the
opinion of high administration officials is shown by Stimson's biographer. It simply did not make sense for Japan to
solve America's most difficult problem and unite the American people overnight. Thus, the attack was not foreseen.

CHAPTER FOUR

THE CONTROVERSY ABOUT GENERAL MARSHALL AND ADMIRAL STARK

The question about the actions of the top military and Naval commanders in Washington prior to the Pearl Harbor attack is most important to an understanding of the controversy surrounding it. Did they perform their duties adequately? Were they asleep at a crucial time? Or were they perhaps part of a conspiracy of silence? It is significant to recall that both the Army Pearl Harbor Board and the Navy Court of Inquiry, as well as the minority of the Joint Congressional Committee, concluded that either the Chief of Staff, or the Chief of Naval Operations, or their subordinates, or all of these, were in part responsible for the disaster. The Roberts Commission, as well as the majority of the congressional committee, disagreed. The stage was set for a dispute that has raged ever since.

The problem of the actions of the chief military and Naval authorities in Washington may be stated fairly simply. Did they send adequate warnings to their subordinates at Hawaii? And if they did, did they exercise the proper supervision to see that their orders were carried out properly? Moreover, what were they doing on Saturday and Sunday, December 6 and 7, and why did they not respond more rapidly and forcefully to the multiplying signs that the outbreak of hostilities was imminent?

Warnings Sent to Hawaii. Just how clearly General Short and Admiral Kimmel were warned of the pending danger has become a highly disputed point. The personal relations between Admirals Stark and Kimmel were close, and throughout the early part of 1941, the Chief of Naval Operations wrote frequent personal letters to the Commander of the Pacific Fleet, as he had to Kimmel's predecessor. On May 27, 1940, Stark explained to Richardson that the fleet had been ordered to Pearl Harbor in order to have a deterrent effect on Japan. On November 12, 1940, the Chief of Naval Operations sent to Admiral Hart at Manila, with a copy to Richardson, a summary predicting a possible Japanese attack on the British and Dutch and cautioning that the United States might also become involved. In his last letter to Richardson as CINCPAC, on December 23, he again emphasized that the Navy must be prepared for war, an injunction he repeated to Kimmel on January 13, 1941. In subsequent letters, he stressed that there was considerable sentiment for action should Japan attack British or Dutch possessions in the Far East and kept Kimmel informed about the worsening political situation between the United States and the island empire. In all these letters, the emphasis was generally on a probable Japanese move toward the Dutch East Indies, Thailand, and Malaya, but the possibility of air attacks against American installations was well known. As early as June 17, 1940, Short's predecessor, Lieutenant General Charles D. Herron, was ordered to go on an immediate alert to deal with a possible trans-Pacific raid. On January 24, 1941, the Secretary of the Navy sent a memorandum to the Secretary of War, with copies to the Commander of the Pacific Fleet, in which he stated that if war started with Japan, "it is believed easily possible that hostilities would be initiated by a surprise attack upon the fleet or the naval base at Pearl Harbor," with air bombing and air torpedo plane attacks ranking first in the order of probability. While Stark on May 14, 1941, wrote to his fleet commanders that an air attack seemed a remote possibility in the Eastern Pacific, he stressed that "we cannot discount it, and hence should... be bending every ounce of effort . . . not to be caught napping in that area."

Short was also warned about a possible air attack. On February 7, 1941, shortly after he reached Fort Shafter, he learned from General Marshall that sabotage and the risk involved in a surprise air attack constituted the real perils to his command at Hawaii. The Chief of Staff repeated the warning on March 5, when he wrote again that the establishment of a satisfactory defense system against an air attack was a matter of first priority. Then, on March 31, Major General Frederick L. Martin, commander of the Army Air Force at Hawaii, and Rear Admiral Patrick N. L. Bellinger, his Naval counterpart, in a joint estimate of the situation, pointed out that in the past Japan had never preceded hostile actions by a declaration of war, and that, therefore, "a successful, sudden raid, against our ships and Naval installations at Oahu" was a possibility. On July 17, the Commanding General of the Army Air Forces in the islands received a memorandum from the Secretary of the Chief of Staff asking him to make a study of the air situation at Hawaii, a memorandum routed through the Commanding General of the Hawaiian Department. The result was a long paper by Martin under the date of August 20, with recommendations covering every conceivable precaution against an air attack, a paper which was endorsed by General Short. Thus both Kimmel and Short had long been aware of the threat of an air attack, although in a warning to Kimmel on October 16 that a Japanese assault on the United States was a decided possibility, there was no mention of it. The Commander of the Pacific Fleet could not have been very startled when on November 25, Stark wrote him that neither the President nor the Secretary of State would be "surprised over a Japanese surprise attack."

Late in November, Kimmel and Short received more specific warnings. On the 24th, the Chief of Naval Operations informed his fleet commanders that chances for a favorable outcome of negotiations with Japan were very doubtful. A surprise aggressive movement in any direction, including an attack on the Philippines or Guam was therefore a possibility. He added that the Chief of Staff concurred and requested that local army commanders be notified. Then, on November 27, following the rejection of the *modus vivendi* and the transmission of Hull's tenpoint note, both Stark and Marshall sent definite war warnings to the American outposts in the Pacific. "This dispatch is to be considered a war warning," read the message to Kimmel, who was informed that an aggressive

movement by Japan was expected within a few days,
most probably against the Philippines, Thailand, the
Kra Isthmus, or Borneo. The admiral was to execute an
appropriate defensive deployment preparatory to carrying
out the tasks assigned in WPL-46 and to alert General
Short. *(See Document No. 24.)* Short likewise received a
telegram from Washington with the intelligence that for
all practical purposes, negotiations with Japan appeared
to be terminated. Hostile Japanese action was possible at
any moment, it warned, but if hostilities could not be
avoided, the United States desired Japan to commit the
first hostile act. The general was to employ such reconnaissance measures as he deemed necessary but he was not
to alarm the civilian population. "Report measures taken,"
the message continued *(see Document No. 25),* and Short,
for reasons never made clear, decided to institute a sabotage alert. This had the effect of causing his planes to be
bunched closely together, thus presenting an excellent
target for the Japanese. He reported his action to his
superiors on the same day.

The Failure to Correct Short's Misapprehensions.
It so happened that on November 27, General Marshall
was away from Washington to supervise maneuvers in
North Carolina. In his absence, the Chief of the Operations Division, Brigadier General Leonard T. Gerow, was
the ranking officer in the War Department charged with
the implementation of orders to commanders in the
field. Not fully comprehending the implication of Short's
reply, he failed to react, and when Marshall returned that
evening, he also missed the significance of Short's answer.
In fact, on the next day, Short received another communication which confirmed his previous assessment. The message alerted him to the danger of subversive activities and
sabotage.

In the week that followed, no further significant *Magic*
information was sent to Hawaii, with the exception of the
code-burning message of December 3 and the final warning on December 7. Neither the deadline messages, nor the
intercepts from Germany, nor the espionage reports were

passed on to the commanders in the islands. As both General Marshall and Admiral Stark explained, they believed sufficient warning had been given on November 27. Kimmel and Short were experienced flag and general officers; they might be expected to know how to deal with an obvious war danger.

It was to be foreseen that this state of affairs would become a major point in the revisionist argument. Even before the Pearl Harbor hearings fully revealed the exact procedure followed in the War Department, John T. Flynn concluded that there was no reaction to the sabotage alert because Roosevelt was maneuvering to have the Japanese fire the first shot in Asia and did not want to do anything that would seem provocative. The minority of the Congressional Committee substantially agreed; it concluded that the warning messages were "couched in such conflicting and imprecise language that they failed to convey to the commanders definite information on the state of diplomatic relations." While the majority differed and held the warnings to have been sufficient, revisionist writers have severely condemned the Washington bureaucracy for its handling of the situation. This is especially significant because even the majority conceded that the handling of Short's reply was careless, and that General Gerow had to bear some of the responsibility for the failure of communications. But of course the principal question must still be answered. Why did the War Department fail to realize the erroneous impression it had created in Hawaii?

Both General Marshall and Admiral Stark sought to explain this riddle. Expecting conferences to be held between the Army and Navy authorities on the ground, both chiefs were convinced that air attacks had been talked about for so long that local commanders would automatically take the necessary steps for defense. If Marshall and Stark stressed sabotage and the necessity of letting Japan fire the first shot, they did so upon the direct request of the President, but neither imagined that this instruction would in any way interfere with preparedness of a more general nature. And of course they were not really thinking of the possibility of an attack on Pearl Harbor. Japan was expected to strike in Southeast Asia, to attack the Dutch East Indies, Malaya, possibly even the Philippines or Guam, but Pearl Harbor seemed unlikely. Obsessed as they were with their concentration of the Southwestern Pacific, they missed the significance of Short's inadequate reply. In fact, General Gerow believed it was merely an acknowledgement of a different message, one from G-2. Thus Marshall, Gerow, and Stark were guilty of negligence, understandable perhaps, but negligence just the same.

What made this situation even worse was the fact that once having decided that sufficient warning had been sent, neither Gerow nor his Naval counterpart, Rear Admiral Richard K. Turner, would allow anyone to deflect them from their course and refused to entertain any suggestions that more information should be forwarded to American commanders overseas. Colonel Sadtler's experience on December 5 with Gerow is a case in point. "I think they have plenty of notification," was Gerow's reply to the request that he send an additional message. Turner, at Naval headquarters, reacted similarly. When Commander McCollum came to him on the same day with a memorandum spelling out all the signals pointing to war and asked that the fleet be alerted, the Admiral showed him the November 24 and 27 warnings. Correcting McCollum's memorandum until it contained very little significant news, he said: "Well, if you want to send it, you either send it the way I corrected it, or take it back to Wilkinson and we will argue about it." The Commander did give it to Captain Wilkinson who kept it. Apparently it was never sent. The net result was that both Kimmel and Short received few further intimations of what was in their superiors' minds or what was going on in Washington and Tokyo.

The Lost Japanese Fleet. Because it was the duty of Naval intelligence to keep track of potentially hostile ships, it is remarkable that starting in the middle of November, American intelligence had no knowledge of the whereabouts of six Japanese carriers and two battleships.

Usually the location of fleet units is determined by radio call signals; the silence maintained by the fleet on its way to attack Pearl Harbor naturally threw off all observers. It was believed that the battleship *Hiyei* was located near Sasebo, the battleship *Kirishima* near Kure, and the carriers *Akagi* and *Kaga* near Kyushu. Four more carriers, the *Soryu, Hiryu, Zuikaku,* and *Shokaku* were assumed to be near Kure. The reason for these alleged locations was that there had been no radio traffic from and to these ships, a fact which led to the assumption that they were in home waters. Apparently, the Naval intelligence service did not have any facilities to deal with vessels that had not been definitely located, and no one seems to have considered the possiblity of their being engaged in unknown offensive operations.

The Reaction to the Fourteen-Point and Related Messages. One of the most controversial episodes of the entire Pearl Harbor affair is the problem of the actions of Marshall, Stark, and their subordinates on December 6 and 7, 1941, the Saturday preceding and the Sunday coinciding with the attack on the American fleet. It was on the 6th that both the Army and Navy obtained the first thirteen parts of the Japanese answer to Hull's ten-point note. The initial portions of this intercept started coming in at about 3:00 p. m. An hour earlier, the pilot message was also intercepted. Colonel Bratton brought it to the attention of Brigadier General Sherman Miles, his superior, and arranged for the usual Army distribution for *Magic* recipients, the Secretary of State, the Chief of Staff, and the Chief of the War Plans Division. After thirteen parts of the fourteen-part message were in, Lieutenant Commander Kramer in turn began to distribute them to the authorized recipients, although he was unable to reach the Chief of Naval Operations. He called Mrs. Kramer, who acted as his chauffeur, and at 9:15 p.m. took the locked pouch with the intercepts to the White House, where he found Lieutenant Schulz taking care of Captain Beardall's office. Then he went to the Wardman Park Hotel to deliver the pouch to the Secretary of the

Navy, who maintained an apartment there. After handing the intercept personally to Knox, he left for Arlington, where Captain Wilkinson's private residence was located. The Captain was giving a dinner party; Beardall and Miles were also present. Later General Miles received a telephone call from Bratton and took full responsibility for notifying the Chief of Staff, while Kramer was driven home for a much needed rest. Where Marshall was that night, and why he did not see the thirteen parts and the pilot message earlier has remained a mystery. Bratton's recollections about the matter were indistinct; at one time he thought the pouch had been put in the hands of Colonel Walter Bedell Smith, the Secretary of the General Staff; later, he believed that it was only delivered the next morning, with the fourteenth part. Marshall himself could not remember; nor did he have any distinct recollection about his whereabouts, although he assumed that he was at home.

Neither Colonel Bratton nor Lieutenant Commander Kramer got much rest that night. The Colonel was back in his office between 7 and 8 o'clock, Sunday morning, and Kramer arrived at his at 7:30 a.m. The fourteenth part arrived shortly afterward, and while the first thirteen parts were not particularly revealing, the fourteenth was couched in undeniably harsh language, concluding with the statement that the Japanese Government considered it impossible to reach an agreement through further negotiations. This caught both Kramer's and Bratton's attention. What really startled the Colonel, however, was the receipt at about 9:00 a.m. of the message directing the Ambassador to submit the reply to the United States at 1:00 p.m. "This immediately stunned me into frenzied activity," he testified later. Its implications were clear. The Japanese were contemplating some drastic move, possibly an attack on some American installation, at 1 o'clock. Frantically, Bratton began to telephone his superiors, including the Chief of Staff at his quarters at Fort Myer. He was able to reach General Miles; Marshall, however, was not available. As was his custom on Sunday mornings, he was taking a horseback ride in the vicinity of the government's experimental farm, the site of the present Pentagon. Bratton told the general's orderly to find him at once, to get assistance if necessary to tell him to go to the nearest phone and call back because an extremely important message had arrived. When Marshall came back from his ride, he was told about the call, took a shower, and returned it. Bratton offered to come to Fort Myer to show him the documents, but the Chief of Staff said not to bother. He was going to his office at the War Department anyway. It was not until 11:25 a.m. that Bratton finally saw him there, reading the fourteen-part note. The Colonel, anxious to call the General's attention to the 1:00 p.m. message, tried to interrupt him, but Marshall refused to listen. Only when he was through did he finally see the 1:00 p.m. intercept. General Miles, Gerow, and an assistant, Colonel Charles W. Bundy, had also arrived, and Marshall, now thoroughly aroused, asked them for their interpretation. Agreeing that it meant some sort of attack at 1:00 p.m., they urged that overseas commanders be notified at once. Marshall picked up the phone to confer with Stark, who thought enough warning had already been given. Upon the insistence of his visitors, however, Marshall proceeded to write by hand a warning that the Japanese were presenting at 1:00 a.m. what amounted to an ultimatum and that they were under orders to destroy their remaining code machines. Just what significance the hour might have he did not know, but he cautioned his subordinates to be on the alert. As he was writing, Stark called back. He had changed his mind and wanted the Navy to be notified. Marshall added a postscript to this effect *(see Document No. 26)* and gave the message to Colonel Bratton for immediate transmittal to all Pacific outposts, including Pearl Harbor.

The Navy, in the meantime, had also been active. When Kramer received the fourteenth part of the long message, he notified McCollum, Wilkinson, and Stark. Then he went to the State Department, where at 10:00 a.m. he gave it to Secretary Knox, who was in conference with Stimson and Hull. Back at the Navy Department twenty minutes later, he saw the 1:00 p.m. message as well as the intercept of the hidden word code specifying, "war with Britain." Rushing to see the Chief of Naval Operations, he found McCollum present and mentioned the tie-up between the time cited and the expected attack in Southeast Asia. But Stark was not particularly impressed with the information. At least he did nothing about it, and later had trouble even remembering where he had been the night before. Kramer left to deliver the new intercept to the State Department, where he remarked, in passing, that 1:00 p.m. at Washington corresponded to 7:30 a.m. at Pearl Harbor. Neither he nor anyone else, however, drew the obvious conclusion. Finally, he made another delivery at the White House and returned to his office.

In spite of all the activity that morning, the communications network broke down. When Colonel Bratton arrived at the Traffic Division of the War Department, the officer in charge, Colonel Edward F. French, first had the message typed so that it was legible. Then he discovered that his office had been out of radio contact with Hawaii since 10:20 a.m., so that he could not raise Honolulu. Considering the alternatives of Naval transmission or commercial wires, he chose the latter. He thought it was the fastest method available and gave the message to Western Union. All this took time; Western Union did not send the message out until 12:18 a.m., and when it arrived at RCA headquarters in Honolulu, it was 7:33 a.m., local time. A motorcyclist was to deliver it to Army headquarters at Fort Shafter; because of the bombing, however, he was delayed, so that the warning did not reach General Short until long after the attack. A scrambler telephone, a device that rendered conversation unintelligible to unauthorized listeners, could have established immediate communications.

This set of unfortunate circumstances has been endlessly discussed. Why did Marshall and Stark suffer from such lapses of memory on this, one of the most important weekends of their lives? And why did the Secretary of the Chief of Staff fail to deliver the pilot and thirteen-point messages to his chief as soon as they were received? Why, moreover, was Smith promoted to lieutenant general while Bratton remained a colonel? And above all, where was Marshall all this time? "In the early hours of the American Revolution," Charles Tansill has written, "Paul Revere went on a famous ride to warn his countrymen of the enemy's approach and thus save American lives. In the early hours of World [War] II, General Marshall took a ride that helped prevent an alert from reaching Pearl Harbor in time to save an American fleet from disaster and an American garrison from a bombing that cost more than 2,000 lives. Was there a more important purpose behind this ride?" The indictment of the Chief of Staff, his associates, and the Chief of Naval Operations has been strengthened by the delays caused by Marshall's late arrival at his office and Stark's failure to be on the alert after the receipt of the 1:00 p.m. message. The disaster of the transmission of the warning message by commercial means has provided further ammunition to Marshall's critics, especially in view of the fact that a scrambler telephone was at hand and the Chief of Staff used it to speak to Short not long after the attack. Admiral Theobald has commented on the inconsistent testimony given by Bratton, and those like Robert H. Ferrell, who have not charged the military and Naval leaders with a conspiracy, have nevertheless cast doubts on their professional competence in this instance.

Of course, there has been no lack of defenders, especially of General Marshall. Forest Pogue, Marshall's biographer, has stressed the fact that the first thirteen points were not in themselves particularly significant; they merely contained the old charges against the United States. In fact, as Pogue has emphasized, Bratton himself did not become alarmed until he saw the 1:00 p.m. message. If Smith received the pouch, it was incomplete, thus resting in Marshall's safe until the fourteenth part came in. As for Admiral Stark, he returned the President's call when he came back from the theater on Saturday night and must have been told of the thirteen parts. According to Pogue, it was impossible for either Marshall or Stark to have been involved in a mammoth conspiracy. Their characters and careers offered the best evidence to the contrary, especially as they were still playing to gain time. Finally, all the participants in the drama, in Washington as well as in American installations overseas, were convinced that the blow, if it should fall, would fall in the Far East. They considered it most unlikely that Japan would be so foolish as to strike at Pearl Harbor.

The matter of the failure to transmit the warning message in time remains. It is easy to explain why Marshall did not use the scrambler telephone. In the normal course of events, a radio message to Hawaii was the safest and most expeditious way of communicating. The Chief of Staff could not know that the Army radio was not functioning. In fact, he sent Bratton back twice to find out if the message had gone out and when it was likely to arrive, and Bratton did not learn of the mishap. Thus the delay can be explained by simple accident. As Roberta Wohlstetter has shown so well, it was human failure and not conspiratorial plotting that caused the disaster of December 7. Nevertheless, the intriguing speculation has continued.

CHAPTER FIVE

THE CONTROVERSY ABOUT ADMIRAL KIMMEL AND GENERAL SHORT

The role of the Army and Navy commanders at Hawaii on December 7, 1941, has naturally become a subject of intense controversy. How could two senior officers of the highest rank, with sophisticated modern equipment at their disposal, have been so unprepared, especially after receiving a warning on November 27 that war was iminent? How could they have failed to alert their ships and troops to the danger? And how could they have neglected to utilize the interceptor devices available to them, particularly the Army's radar, the Navy's patrol ships, and the reconnaissance planes? These failures seemed so staggering that they too have given rise to theories of foul play, the more so because after the disaster both Admiral Kimmel and General Short were cast in the role of scapegoats. Retired from active service, they were asked to sign waivers for future courts martial, proceedings that were never actually initiated. In time, both commanders became more and more convinced that they had been the victims of a gigantic conspiracy, an alleged plot their defenders have been magnifying ever since.

The actual facts in the case as shown by the available evidence are again fairly simple. For more than ten months prior to the attack, both commanders were fully aware of the danger of air raids. Shortly after his arrival in Hawaii, on January 27, 1941, Admiral Kimmel wrote to the Chief of Naval Operations that he was particularly upset about the lack of Army equipment for the task of protecting the Naval base and expressed the opinion that "the supply of an adequate number of Army planes and guns for the defense of Pearl Harbor should be given the highest priority." On February 18, he added that the need for Army anti-aircraft guns should also be stressed. ". . . surprise attack (submarines, air, or combined) on Pearl Harbor is a definite possibility," he pointed out, and on March 28, the Army and Navy at Hawaii concluded a joint agreement spelling out their individual and mutual responsibilities in case of an air assault. The purpose of the arrangement was "to coordinate joint defensive measures for the security of the fleet and for the Pearl Harbor Naval Base for defense against hostile raids or air attacks delivered prior to a declaration of war." Assaults upon hostile vessels were to be under the command of the Navy, defensive air operations over Oahu under the tactical command of the Army. Three days later, General Martin and Admiral Bellinger drew up a joint estimate of the situation which emphasized that in the past Japan had never preceded hostile actions by a declaration of war. "A successful, sudden raid, against our ships and Naval installations on Oahu might prevent effective offensive action by our forces in the Western Pacific for a long period," they surmised. Specifying a surprise air attack on Oahu as a possible enemy action, they characterized it as the "most likely and dangerous form of attack," presumably to be "launched from one or more carriers which would probably approach inside of three hundred miles."

Kimmel showed that he continued to worry about the safety of the fleet in various communications to his friend, Admiral Stark, whom he, like all those who knew the Chief of Naval Operations intimately, called Betty. On May 26, he complained that the defense of the fleet base at Pearl Harbor was a matter of major concern, and that pressure ought to be brought upon the Army to get more anti-aircraft guns, airplanes, and radar equipment for use at Hawaii. He continued to stress the importance of radar facilities, particularly sensors that were able to differentiate between friend and foe, and asked for additional personnel, ships, and equipment.

Short was also aware of the danger. Not long after arriving at his new post at Fort Shafter, he wrote to the Chief of Staff that, in order "to meet an attack from any direction," he considered the dispersion and protection of aircraft and the improvement of anti-aircraft and harbor defense artillery of major importance. After a warning from Marshall on May 5 to review the situation with regard to protection against air attack, he submitted a long summary stating that in this connection the vulnerability of both Army and Navy airfields constituted the most acute difficulty. Pointing out that on all landing facilities the planes had been kept "lined up on the field where they would suffer terrific loss," he concluded that defense against air raids was his most serious problem. Of course, he was fully aware of the Martin-Bellinger estimate, and on May 29, reported the successful conclusion of maneuvers presupposing an attack on an aircraft carrier 250 miles out at sea.

Failure to Take War Warnings Seriously. Notwithstanding these preparations, by the fall, both Kimmel and Short seemingly disregarded the most elementary precautions against air attack. Believing that whatever danger existed affected a geographic area far removed from Hawaii — Malaya, the Dutch East Indies, or Thailand — Kimmel was confirmed in this misjudgment by a message from Stark on October 16. It warned of the probability of war but directed Pacific naval commanders to take all precautions "including such preparatory deployments as will not disclose strategic intention nor constitute provocative actions against Japan." Kimmel was not even particularly aroused by the specific warnings he received on November 27. Although Stark's message clearly identified it as a war warning and directed appropriate defense measures, the admiral, convinced that the Southwest Pacific was the area chiefly endangered, continued to conduct training exercises much as before. Simultaneous orders to send carriers with Army planes to Wake and Midway Islands further concentrated his attention to locations other than Hawaii. As Peter Herde has pointed out, in view of the danger of premature discovery, a Japanese surprise attack on Oahu appeared too illogical to be taken seriously. Not even when Kimmel learned that the Japanese were buring their codes did he believe that in his command there was need for additional precautions. Everything seemed to point toward action in the southwestern Pacific, thousands of miles to the west. At Hawaii, sabotage appeared to be the principal danger.

It is true that even had Kimmel wanted to institute an effective aerial reconnaissance patrol, he did not have enough planes for that purpose. The only patrol that could have provided the proper protection for an island like Oahu would have necessitated a twenty-four hour reconnaissance on a 360° radius to a distance of 800 miles, a task requiring 84 planes every sixteen hours, 250 planes altogether, far more than could have been assembled at Hawaii. Yet the fact remains that Kimmel made few attempts to utilize even the planes he had.

Short may be faulted in similar fashion. Taking a cue from the Army Pearl Harbor Board, in his later testimony he called Marshall's November 27 warning the "Do-Don't" message." It directed him not to alarm the civilian population; consequently, he merely instituted a sabotage alert, the lowest state of alarm. When he reported this action to Washington, General Gerow's failure to correct him naturally confirmed Short in his mistaken assessment of the situation, and he continued to keep his troops on the low sabotage alert. Because he did not receive any further messages about the *Magic* intercepts, and because the Navy did not completely share its intelligence with him, he was not kept fully informed about the actual state of the negotiations. However, he knew that the Japanese-American talks had virtually come to an end; the newspapers were printing more and more alarming headlines every morning.

Kimmel and the Lost Fleet. Naval intelligence at Hawaii as well as at Washington was in the dark about the location of the Japanese battleships and carriers which for some time had observed radio silence. When in his written summary on December 1, Lieutenant Commander Edwin T. Layton, Kimmel's intelligence officer, specifically pointed out that the change after only one month in the Japanese service call signs was as indication of "additional progressive steps in preparing for active operations on a large scale," Kimmel underlined this sentence in pencil and asked Layton to prepare a location sheet on the Japanese navy. Receiving it the next day, he remarked that the missing carriers were not indicated. "What? You don't know where Carrier Division 1 and Carrier Division 2 are? he said. Upon Layton's reply that they were probably in home waters but that he could not be sure, the Admiral remarked: "Do you mean they could be rounding Diamond Head and you wouldn't know it?" The intelligence specialist answered that he hoped they would be sighted before reaching Hawaii. Nevertheless, Kimmel, whose intelligence service had lost elements of the Japanese fleet in the past, was not so disturbed about this fact as to redouble his reconnaissance efforts.

Additional Last Minute Warnings. Although the November 27 war warning had not resulted in a full alert at Hawaii, there were a few last minute alarms that might ordinarily have jolted the local commanders out of their complacency. One of these was the Mori call. This telephone conversation between someone in Tokyo and Dr. Motokazu Mori in Honolulu, who mentioned various airplane movements, anti-aircraft measures, and items of military interest in Hawaii, as well as various flowers in bloom, was intercepted by the FBI and given to Naval and military intelligence. *(See Document No. 27.)* Colonel George W. Bicknell, the Assistant G-2, immediately called his superior, Colonel Fielder, who was just about to go to dinner with Short, to alert him and the General. Fielder told Bicknell to be at Fort Shafter within the next ten minutes; Bicknell promptly arrived and found both Fielder and Short, who had waited for him. Showing them the Mori call, he said that he considered it highly suspicious and significant. The General, with his G-2 looking over his shoulder, read the message. But they were not impressed with it. In fact, Bicknell had the feeling that they thought him a bit too intelligence conscious.

If Short did not react to the Mori call, he might at least have taken note of the fact that the Japanese consulate was burning its secret papers. Bicknell had pointed out this information at that morning's staff conference. But the tip made no more impression on the General than all the other indications of approaching war. He was convinced that they all had reference to the Far East.

The Navy soon received even more alarming warnings. Early on Sunday morning, the destroyer *Ward* acknowledged a signal from the mine sweeper *Condor* that a submarine had been sighted in the closed waters near the entrance to Pearl Harbor. Because of the darkness, the *Ward* was unable to find the intruder. At 6:40 a.m., however, it also discovered a submarine, one which was attempting to follow the *Antares* toward the narrow passage leading to the fleet anchorage. Commander William W. Outerbridge, the captain of the *Ward,* gave orders to attack and within a short time sank the submarine with depth charges. This incident was immediately reported to the District Watch Officer, who was alone and at first unable to reach the aide of Admiral Claude C. Bloch, commandant of the Fourteenth Naval District. When the watch officer finally succeeded in alerting his superiors, including Kimmel, they first tried to verify the report about the submarine, followed as it was by one about the capture of a sampan in forbidden waters which the *Ward* was taking to Honolulu. These verification efforts were still going on when the attack started. *(See Document No. 28.)*

In addition, prior to Pearl Harbor the two services at Hawaii failed to establish effective systems of cooperation. Admiral Kimmel did not know that General Short had three types of alert, of which No. 1 was the lowest, and intelligence messages, such as the ones about the Japanese order to destroy various codes, were not routinely exchanged between the Navy and the Army.

Finally, Short's failure to use his radar properly has often been criticized. Radar was then of fairly recent origin, and the army did not have sufficient trained personnel to man the installations properly. A mobile unit had been installed at Opana, in the extreme north of Oahu. General Short's orders specified that on weekends it was to be in operation between 4:00 and 7:00 a.m., a time which he considered most likely for an air attack. Lacking spare parts and not expecting an air raid in any case, the General decided that the three hours' operation was warranted. As it happened that Sunday morning, however, two enlisted men, Specialist 3d Class Joseph L. Lockard and Private George E. Elliott, Jr., who had been operating the mobile unit during the assigned hours, kept working a little longer, both to obtain more practice and to await the truck which was supposed to pick them up at 7:30 a.m. At 7:02 a.m., they suddenly saw a large number of planes approaching from the northwest. Still about 136 miles away, the planes constituted the largest radar blip that either Lockard or Elliot had ever seen. Accordingly, they called the information center to report their discovery. At first, they found no one at the other end of the so-called tactical line; then, trying a different phone, they raised the operator who initially did not know what to do about the information. In the end, he reached the lone officer on duty at the center, Lieutenant Kermit A. Tyler, who returned the call. Learning about the sighting, he recalled that he had heard Hawaiian music played on the radio all night long, an indication, he knew, that was often used by bomber pilots coming from the West Coast for homing. Thus, he concluded that the two soldiers had seen the image of the expected flight of B-17's which had been ordered to Hawaii and he told Lockard and Elliott not to worry. The two soldiers continued to observe the planes a little longer, until they were about thirty miles distant. Then Lockard and Elliott left. Another sure indication of impending disaster was missed. *(See Document No. 29.)*

These facts have led various commentators to draw the most contradictory conclusions. "Had I known, as the record plainly shows, that from August until December 7, 1941, the administration's policy was to enter the war through an incident in the Pacific or, as the Secretary of State put it, to induce Japan to fire the first shot without too much injury to overselves, my whole concept of the situation would have been considerably altered," Admiral Kimmel wrote in his memoirs. Arguing that he did not have the information he needed to make proper dispositions, the Admiral concluded that, had he been aware of the *Magic* intercepts, particularly the "bomb plot" and ships-in-harbor messages, he would have rejected the Navy Department's instructions to send carriers to Wake and Midway. Instead, he would have ordered the *Saratoga* to return from the West Coast, and, in order to be ready to meet an attack, taken the fleet to sea. Admiral Theobald, his chief defender, has not only backed him up, but has insisted that the required information was deliberately withheld so that the fleet would not leave port and deprive the Japanese of a target. Short substantially agreed with his colleague. Especially indignant about the War Department's failure to correct his mistaken response to the war warning, he maintained that he would have made an entirely different estimate of the situation had he been given the proper information.

Even though shortly after the disaster the Roberts Commission put much of the blame on Kimmel and Short, the Army Pearl Harbor Board and the Navy Court of Inquiry partially exonerated them. Finding that the General failed to place his command in a state of readiness for war, as has been shown, the Army Board, nevertheless, also blamed Short's superiors in Washington for not keeping him sufficiently informed about the *Magic* intercepts. The Navy Court of Inquiry went further. It concluded that "in view of the Chief of Naval Operations' approval of the precautions taken and the deployment made by Admiral Kimmel in accordance with the directive contained in the dispatch of 16 October, 1941 . . . Admiral Kimmel's decision, made after receiving the dispatch of 24 November, to continue preparations of the Pacific Fleet for war, was sound in the light of the information then available to him." No wonder that Peter Herde, otherwise critical of Kimmel, believes that in view of the omissions in Washington any other commander would have been similarly surprised, and that Bruce Bartlett roundly condemns the "petty" effort to blame Kimmel and Short for the disaster.

In spite of these factors, however, the two commanders have been unable to escape censure. Not even the minority of the Pearl Harbor Committee absolved them from all

guilt, and their evident shortcomings have been repeatedly pointed out. After all, they did receive a war warning;
they did have radar, and they failed to coordinate their
efforts properly. To allow the radar operation not only
to be understaffed but also to remain in the hands of ill-
trained personnel was an error Short could not deny, and
to refuse to take seriously the inability to locate most of
Japan's carriers without, after the war warning, instituting
a more thorough reconnaissance, was equally irresponsible
on Kimmel's part. Although both officers had distinguished careers behind them, and in many ways, were the
victims of circumstances over which they had little control, their overall performance, viewed in retrospect,
leaves much to be desired. They were, as Roberta Wohlstetter has stated, simply "not tuned to the reception
of danger signals."

CHAPTER SIX

THE CONTROVERSY ABOUT JAPAN'S STRATEGY AND HER COLLABORATION WITH GERMANY

The origins of the plan to attack Pearl Harbor are hardly in dispute. It has been conceded generally that it was first conceived by Admiral Yamamoto sometime in the beginning of 1941, although David Bergamini credits the Imperial House with a greater part in the scheme than the facts warrant. Made aware of the possibility of aerial torpedo attacks upon naval vessels in shallow waters by the success in November, 1940 of the British assault upon the Italians at Taranto, the Admiral believed a similar attack upon the American Navy would be feasible. Of course, the plan involved great risks; a carrier fleet would have to sail unnoticed to within about 250 miles of the target, and Yamamoto's colleagues in the admiralty could not see how he dared risk his carriers so nonchalantly, or how he could refuel the task force once it was at sea. As time went on, however, all these obstacles were overcome, and after extensive exercises in Kagoshima Bay, the Admiral was more than ever convinced of the feasibility of his project. Yet it was not until after he threatened the Chief of the Naval Staff, Osami Nagano, with his intention to resign, that on November 3, Yamamoto finally secured the adoption of his daring scheme. Within a few weeks, his task force assembled in fog-enshrouded Hitokappu Bay, from where it sailed on its mission on November 26. Another task force, consisting of submarines and a few midget subs, also gathered for cooperation with the main fleet.

Reasons for Japan's Decision to Attack. Why Japan decided to strike at Hawaii and challenge the United States is a significant question. After the war, most American observers agreed that the attackers had committed a major blunder. As soon as he heard of the raid, Secretary of War Stimson wrote in his diary that upon learning the news his first feeling was one of relief that the indecision was over and "that a crisis had come in a way which would unite all our people." In fact, the Japanese did unite isolationists and interventionists, Republicans and Democrats, friends and foes of the President. So successful were the attackers in unifying the American people that Roosevelt's opponents have long wondered whether the entire course of events was not deliberately planned by the administration. Moreover, the American fleet could not operate more than 2,000 miles from its base, so that it could not have materially interfered with Japan's military advance toward the south. Instead of attempting to sink the American warships on the high seas, the enemy actually sent them to the bottom at their Naval base, where they could be raised again and repaired. In addition, Yamamoto had been especially anxious to destroy the carriers, but as luck would have it, none were at the base when the raid occurred. The *Enterprise,* accompanied by three heavy cruisers and nine destroyers, was on its way to Wake Island; the *Lexington,* accompanied by three heavy cruisers and five destroyers, was sailing toward Midway, and the *Saratoga* had been sent to the West Coast for repairs. Other carriers were not even in the Pacific, so that the raid was less than a complete success. Had the Japanese heeded Hitler's advice and left the United States alone, they might have solved their problems without formal American entry into the war.

All in all, the returning Japanese raiders were hailed as victors. They had crippled the American Pacific Fleet; as Peter Herde has pointed out, the simultaneous move toward the south took place and was successful; Imperial forces in record time conquered Malaya, Singapore, Hong Kong, the Philippines, Guam, Wake Island, Burma, and, most important of all, the Dutch East Indies. At least for the time being, the greater part of the American Pacific fleet had been crippled. Moreover, the unexpected attainment of total surprise, and the Americans' failure to credit the Japanese with the ability to strike at such a distance, was a great boon to Japanese morale. "The Japanese people in the early days of the war were generally intoxicated with victory, and the feeling was widespread that the years of suffering could be permanently consigned to oblivion," wrote Foreign Minister Shigenori Togo. In fact, this feeling was hardly astonishing.

The decision to attack the United States was due to the widespread belief that any Japanese assault on British posessions in the Far East or the Netherlands East Indies would inevitably bring in the Americans. An advance to the south would have to be supplied by water; unwilling to take this risk as long as there was an American fleet in being in the Pacific, Yamamoto convinced his colleagues that it would be advantageous for Japan to strike at the fleet first, thus removing the dagger he believed pointed at the very heart of Japan. This plan involved the complete reversal of Japanese naval doctrine, which had always presupposed the destruction of American fleet units in waters nearer home, but it did have the advantage of being totally unexpected, in fact, so much so that its very daring made it impossible for the Americans to consider it a serious possibility. To succeed completely, however, as T.R. Fehrenbach and others have shown, the attackers would have had to destroy installations on shore, especially the oil tanks and repair facilities. Had they done so, it is difficult to see how the United States could have recovered as quickly as it did, and Admiral Chichi Nagumo, the commander of the task force, has been serverely criticized for not staging a third assault after two waves of attacking planes had returned to their carriers. He later explained that he did so because of the satisfaction with the damage already inflicted, the surprising strength of American anti-aircraft fire, the existence of fifty American planes that were still operational, and his ignorance about the whereabouts of the carriers which he had vainly been seeking. In fact, it is difficult to blame him for his decision. He had been so lucky that he did not dare challenge fortune once again.

Much has been written about Yamamoto's alleged boast that he would dictate peace at the White House. Far from envisaging a complete defeat of the United States, the Admiral, unlike many of his colleagues, was fully aware of America's tremendous strength. As a matter of fact, he was certain that, unless Japan could attain a negotiated settlement within two years, disaster threatened. As he allegedly said to Prince Konoye, "If you tell me that it is necessary that we fight, then in the first six months to a year of war against the U.S. and England I will run wild, and I will show you an uninterrupted succession of victories; I must also tell you that should the war be prolonged for two or three years, I have no confidence in our ultimate victory." The Admiral proved as astute in his predictions of grand strategy as he was in planning the Pearl Harbor attack.

The reasons for Japan's decision to strike have generally been condemned as militaristic. The Empire, it has been asserted, was in the grip of an expansionist, unscrupulous military machine which sought to benefit to the utmost from the disaster brought upon the world by Hitler's aggression. Moreover, the Japanese were determined to conquer China and to impose their will upon that country. The various incidents of Japanese terrorism starting in the early thirties, the conquest of Manchuria, and the inhuman type of warfare in China have been cited as examples. Thus, the Empire's refusal to come to terms with the United States has often been pictured as a sheer case of aggression without mitigating circumstances.

The Japanese view of the situation, and that of many modern scholars, is less simplistic. Japan, it is said, had no choice. Deprived of the necessary raw materials by America's ever tightening trade embargoes, she had to act. Because the European powers as well as the United States had long benefited from imperialist adventures in Asia as well as elsewhere, it was not unreasonable for Japan to challenge them in the Far East. In recent years, New Left writers have presented an image of two imperialisms confronting each other, generally to the detriment of the United States. Because the Empire had long invested enormous sums of money, as well as manpower and prestige in the so-called China Incident, it was unrealistic, it has been argued, for the United States to seek to deprive Japan of her rewards by insisting upon a complete withdrawal from China. In retrospect, of course, it is clear that

Japan gained nothing from her adventure and might have been much better off had she left the United States alone, although David Lu argues that it became a blessing for her because it was "the beginning to the end of a military domination." In 1941, however, such views were not popular in Tokyo. On the contrary, it was widely believed that the time to strike was then or the Empire would not survive.

Degree of Knowledge of the Attack. When Kurusu and Nomura presented their fourteen-point note to Secretary Hull, he was firmly convinced that they had betrayed him. "I must say, " he told the Ambassadors, "that in all my conversations with you during the last nine months I have never uttered one word of untruth. This is borne out absolutely by the record. In all my fifty years of public service I have never seen a document that was more crowded with falsehoods and distortions on a scale so huge that I never imagined until today that any Government on this planet was capable of uttering them." Because he received the Ambassadors more than an hour after the first bombs fell on Pearl Harbor, his reaction was not surprising.

Neither Kurusu nor Nomura, however, had the faintest notion of the reason for their orders to present the note at 1:00 p.m. In fact, they dawdled to such a degree that it was not ready at the appointed time. Because of the injunction of secrecy, they were not permitted to employ regular typists, and the inexpert assistant who typed the clean copy for presentation was not able to complete it before one o'clock. Nor were they the only ones who had not been told about the impending attack. Although Gordon W. Prange has shown that the circle of Yamamoto's initiates was not small, the secret was so well guarded that members of the cabinet in Tokyo only learned of it at the beginning of December. In fact, General Tojo himself was kept in the dark about many of the details. This secrecy was unquestionably necessary; without it, the operation could not have succeeded.

German-Japanese Collaboration. During the Second World War, it was generally believed that Germany and

Japan were acting in close concert. The Rome-Berlin-Tokyo Axis was regarded as an evident conspiracy of aggressors whose evil purposes were obviously coordinated. That this was not true has long been known. Actually, the strains between Japan and Germany often outweighed the two countries' capacity for cooperation, and the events leading to Pearl Harbor clearly illustrate this fact.

It is not to be denied that the Nazis were overjoyed when they learned about the raid. They were totally surprised at the intelligence; von Ribbentrop at first thought it was an enemy propaganda trick and was annoyed at having been awakened because of it. When the news was confirmed, however, both von Ribbentrop and Hitler were wholly satisfied. Convinced that Japan had acted in the best interests of the Axis, the dictator slapped his thighs in sheer delight and expounded on the new world situation. Later on, he explained that Japan had come in just at the right time. Her entry was a great boost to German morale, already shaken because of the Wehrmacht's difficulties in Russia. Reassured by the hated Americans' defeat, on December 8, he ordered his navy to fire upon all American flag ships and on December 11, declared war upon the United States.

This peculiar action — according to the provisions of the Tripartite Pact he might well have stayed on the sidelines because Japan had initiated the hostilities — has been severely criticized. Gerhard Weinberg has called attention to the fact that Hitler declared war without any sort of consultation with his advisers, without any discussion, and seemingly without any thought of the consequences. Others have shown that it made any further isolationist activity in America impossible and finally solved Roosevelt's most persistent obstacle to aiding Great Britain. In truth, it contradicted the *Führer's* long held idea of keeping the United States on the sidelines if at all possible, a reversal which was astounding. But his eagerness for a new ally to offset his losses on the Russian front rendered him incautious.

It is true that Germany's attitude toward the Japanese-American negotiations had always been negative. Worried about the possibility of an agreement between the two Pacific powers at their expense, the Nazis constantly cautioned their treaty partners against alleged American machinations. They sought to induce the Japanese to attack Singapore, and, after opening hostilities with Russia, suggested an assault on Vladivostok as well. As for the United States, they either underestimated its strength or sought to convince the Japanese to leave America alone for the time being.

The Japanese in turn hoped to benefit from their connection with the Axis. Following Germany's defeat of France, they imposed their onerous conditions on Marshall Pétain. Matsuoka, in fact, intended to go further, and after Germany's attack on the Soviet Union, favored parallel Japanese operations. But because of their immediate need for raw materials, the Japanese abandoned for the moment any thought of moving north. Matsuoka fell, and the negotiations with America continued. Moreover, when the Japanese made contingency plans for an eventual attack on the United States, they carefully concealed their intentions from their ally. As Professor Herde has shown, as late as October, 1941, the Tokyo authorities, falsely making the German Ambassador in Tokyo believe that he could ignore the possibility of a war with America altogether, deliberately misled him.

With the collapse of the Hull-Nomura conversations, however, the situation changed. Now anxious to secure German cooperation, the Tojo government must have been happy to learn that von Ribbentrop had become more favorably disposed toward a war with the United States. At ten thirty in the evening of November 28, he saw the Japanese Ambassador in Berlin, General Hiroshi Oshima. Asking Oshima about the progress of negotiations with America, the Foreign Minister remarked that he thought it essential for Japan to effect the "new order" in Asia. Because there were fundamental differences "in the very right to exist" between Germany and Japan on

the one side and the United States on the other, and
because the Japanese-American conversations appeared to
have no chance of success, a Japanese decision to fight the
United States would be in the interest of Germany as well
as of Japan. Astonished at this reversal, Oshima asked
whether a state of war was to be established between Germany and the United States. Von Ribbentrop now re-
treated a little. "Roosevelt's a fanatic, so it is impossible
to tell what he would do," he said. Oshima concluded that
Germany's attitude had hardened, not only because of
von Ribbentrop's remarks, but also because of a bellicose
speech Hitler had delivered. "There are indications at present that Germany would not refuse to fight if necessary,"
he reported to Tokyo. *(See Document No. 30.)*

Shortly afterward, he finally received binding instructions from Tokyo. The Foreign Minister wired that the
Hull-Nomura conversations were ruptured and asked
Oshima to see Hitler and von Ribbentrop to inform them
of this development. In addition, he was to make it clear
to them that "war may suddenly break out between the
Anglo-Saxon nations and Japan through some clash of
arms and . . . that the time of the breaking out of this
war may come quicker than anyone dreams." *(See Document No. 31.)* These messages from and to the Japanese
embassy in Berlin were intercepted by *Magic*.

Oshima soon received more detailed orders. Recalled
from a Mozart festival in Vienna, on December 2 he found
instructions to ask for more binding agreements with
Germany. What Tokyo had in mind was an expansion of
the Tripartite Pact to make it offensive as well as defensive. In addition, the Japanese wanted a no-separate-peace
agreement with the Germans. The Ambassador immediately complied with these directives. But as Hitler was not
in Berlin, von Ribbentrop delayed answering the Japanese
requests, and it was not until three o'clock in the morning
of December 5 that he summoned Oshima. The German
Foreign Minister accepted the proposed revision of the
treaty and agreed to a new text incorporating the unconditional alliance as well as to a no-separate-peace agreement. Because the new arrangements had not yet been

formally completed, however, and the attack on Pearl Harbor was planned for the 7th, Togo again wired Oshima on the 6th to make certain that, pending the completion of formalities, the agreement was indeed in force. Worried about possible German demands for participation in the war against the Soviet Union, the Foreign Minister also asked the Ambassador to make sure the Nazis understood that at present the Empire was unable to attack Russia. If Germany did not agree to this condition, the signing of the pact would have to be postponed.

Hitler, however, had no objections. Pleased that Japan had finally decided to strike, he did not require her to come to his assistance against the Soviet Union. And although the new pact had not yet been signed by December 7, he honored it by declaring war against the United States. If Japan had committed a blunder, Germany, along with Italy, which also declared war, had merely compounded it.

CHAPTER SEVEN

CONCLUSION

Whether the controversy about the Pearl Harbor attack will ever be settled is doubtful. But a few salient facts seem to have emerged from all the discussion and research. In the first place, it is evident that Franklin D. Roosevelt, convinced of the necessity of Allied victory, was anxious to aid Great Britain to the utmost extent of his ability. Fully aware of the constitutional limitations governing his powers to act but baffled by the isolationist opposition, he went as far as he could in resisting the Germans without actually going to war. The modification of the Neutrality Act in November 1939, the destroyer deal, the Lend-Lease Act, the occupation of Greenland and Iceland, the freezing of Axis funds, and the shoot-on-sight orders are all examples of this endeavor, which was finally crowned by the November 1941 revision of the Neutrality Act. But Hitler did not respond.

That Roosevelt deliberately sought to provoke Japan in order to enter the war by the "back door" cannot be proven. Considering the island empire a real threat to the United States and an active ally of the hated Nazis, he sought by all means possible to curb its expansionism. The maintenance of the Open Door in China had been a time-honored American policy going back to the beginning of the century; the strong China Lobby in the State Department as well as the friends of Chiang Kai-shek in high places knew how to keep sympathy for their cause alive. In view of the Armed Forces' warning that they were not ready for hostilities and that the President ought to attempt to gain time, it is unlikely that he consciously pushed Japan into war. On the contrary, both he and Secretary of State Cordell Hull seem to have felt that economic pressure would cause Japan to desist. When they realized their policy was not working it was too late to pull back. Although staff conversations with Great Britain and the Netherlands had provided for common action in case the Japanese invaded certain parts of

Southeast Asia, including Thailand, Malaya, and the Dutch East Indies, these agreements were not binding on the United States. The President had never affixed his signature to them.

Under these circumstances, accusations that Roosevelt "baited" the Japanese are unconvincing. It is true that the order to send out three small ships from Manila on the eve of the war looks suspicious, but without clear proof to the contrary, it would appear to have been a mere effort on the part of the administration, fumbling to be sure, to obtain more information about Japanese operations in the South China Sea. Even modern revisionists no longer maintain that the fleet was deliberately exposed at Pearl Harbor to provide Japan with a worthwhile target. The President loved the Navy too much to sacrifice it so callously; moreover, there is absolutely no evidence that in the fall of 1941 anyone, either in Washington or in Hawaii, ever considered an attack on the base a possibility. All signs pointed to a Japanese advance toward the south; Japan's need for oil was well understood, and petroleum was to be found in the Dutch East Indies. Thus the three little vessels were dispatched into the South China Sea; the Australians understood the Dutch to have concluded the (unsigned) staff agreements pertaining to the Southeast Asia were in effect, and Admiral Hart at Manila heard similar news from Captain Creighton.

It is also untrue that the Washington authorities intercepted definite signs of the planned raid clearly pointing to Pearl Harbor. To be sure, the "bomb plot" and ships-in-harbor messages had been deciphered; to be sure they requested minute information about the American fleet from Japanese spies on Oahu, but at the same time, they did not at first seem as important as they appeared afterward. Similar messages had been intercepted elsewhere; West Coast installations and the defenses of the Panama Canal had also been the focus of minute Japanese inquiries. Perhaps this circumstance explains the fact that many of these messages, sent in less complicated codes than *Purple,* were not translated and decrypted until weeks after their receipt. As for the much debated Winds-Execute signal, it does not seem to have been received in proper form prior to December 7, even though Captain Safford thought so. At any rate, its interception would not have altered the facts already known in Washington. Moreover, the realization that the fleet was incapable of strong offensive operations further than 2,000 miles from its home base tended to reinforce the notion that a Japanese attack on Pearl Harbor was not a serious possibility.

All this is not to say that no fateful mistakes were made in Washington. The failure of the Chief of Staff and the Chief of Naval Operations to warn their subordinates properly is inexcusable. No matter how security conscious they were, no matter how concerned they may have been about safeguarding the secret of America's ability to read the Japanese diplomatic code, they cannot escape responsibility for not acting more vigorously after the rejection of the *modus vivendi*. It was not sufficient to send a war warning to Pearl Harbor; the evident intensification of the danger of conflict in the nine days following November 27 should have caused both Marshall and Stark to take every precaution to see to it that all American Pacific commands were in a proper state of readiness. Especially surprising is the failure of the War Plans Division to take note of the fact that General Short had ordered merely a sabotage alert. Immediate instructions to rectify the situation should have been issued, regardless of any danger to the security of the *Magic* intercepts. In addition, on the day before the attack the receipt of the pilot message and the fourteen-point reply should most certainly have persuaded both the War and Navy Departments to go on a full alert, staff their offices to the utmost, and be prepared for every contingency. If on receipt of the news of the Japanese reply the President of the United States could conclude that it meant war, so could the Chief of Staff, the Chief of Naval Operations, and their subordinates. Thus, there is simply no justification for both Marshall's and Stark's heedless actions on December 7, and certainly none for the Chief of

Staff's absence from his office while taking a horseback ride. The last minute warning should have been sent two hours earlier, and the message center should never have been authorized to use commercial communications with their known drawbacks.

These oversights by no means diminish the culpability of the local commanders in Hawaii. As senior officers with a distinguished record in the service, neither Kimmel nor Short can really shield themselves behind the errors of the Navy and War Departments. They were responsible for the safety of their commands. At a time when every newspaper headline proclaimed the imminence of war, they could hardly afford to allow themselves to be surprised in the way they were. They could not defend their failure to use their radar facilities properly; they had no excuse for not conducting more effective reconnaissance; they could not explain their inability to account for most of the potentially hostile carriers, and they could not give any good reasons for their lack of proper warning systems. After the sighting of the first submarines within the security zone, for example, the entire command should have been alerted immediately, and the fact that the Japanese consul in Honolulu was destroying his codes and burning his papers should have given additional cause for vigilance. Neither the Army nor the Navy reacted in a responsible manner, and although the later treatment of Kimmel and Short was not justified, their lack of foresight was certainly a matter for censure.

Finally, there are some answers to the larger strategic questions in connection with Japan's collaboration with Germany. As it has been pointed out, although Pearl Harbor constituted a great tactical victory for the Axis, it also marked the beginning of the Fascists' downfall. By attacking the United States in the way she did, Japan unified the country. Isolationists rallied to the flag; the national cohesion which had for so long escaped the President was forged in an instant, and the tremendous strength of the United States, economic, political, and military, could be brought into full play against the Axis. The

Japanese delusion of a possibility within a short time of forcing the United States to sign a compromise peace was a grave miscalculation, as was the assumption of certain German victory in Russia. As for the Nazis, their initial policy of attempting to keep America as neutral as possible for as long as possible was best calculated to serve their ends. Their efforts to induce the Japanese to attack either the British at Singapore of the Russians at Vladivostok might also have been useful for them. Their reversal of policy in respect to the United States, however, their handing a blank check to the Japanese, constituted a grave error. If Japan could not afford to take on the industrial and military might of the giant on the other side of the Pacific, neither could Germany, then already deeply involved in an increasingly difficult campaign in Russia and still unable to subdue Great Britain. Hitler might have refused to join in the war against the United States, thus enabling the isolationists at least to deflect America's energies to the Pacific. But, blinded by his own propaganda and prejudice, he decided that he needed the boost of Japanese participation in the war effort more than a tenuous state of non-belligerency with the United States. Perhaps the Italian interpreter who was asked to translate the request for a declaration of war on the United States was more prescient than his masters. He trembled like a leaf.

Thus, the Pearl Harbor attack was an operation compounded by errors on all sides. It does not seem to have been the result of any secret plots (except for Yamamoto's well-prepared plan) but appears to have succeeded because of errors in Washington and at Pearl Harbor. The greatest error of all, however, was committed in Tokyo. It was the decision to challenge the might of the United States.

Part II

DOCUMENTS

Document No. 1

THE TRIPARTITE PACT[1]

The Tripartite Pact between Germany, Italy, and Japan was concluded at Berlin on September 27, 1940. Obviously directed against the United States, it became a major stumbling block during the conversations between Secretary of State Cordell Hull and Ambassador Kichisaburo Nomura.

γ   γ   γ

The Governments of Germany, Italy, and Japan consider it as a condition precedent of a lasting peace, that each nation of the world be given its own proper place. They have therefore decided to stand together and to cooperate with one another in their efforts in Greater East Asia and in the regions of Europe wherein it is their prime purpose to establish and maintain a new order of things calculated to promote the prosperity and welfare of the peoples there. Furthermore, it is the desire of the three Governments to extend this cooperation to such nations in other parts of the world as are inclined to give to their endeavor a direction similar to their own, in order that their aspiration towards world peace as the ultimate goal may thus be realized. Accordingly, the Governments of Germany, Italy, and Japan have agreed as follows:

Article 1

Japan recognizes and respects the leadership of Germany and Italy in the establishment of a new order in Europe.

Article 2

Germany and Italy recognize and respect the leadership of Japan in the establishment of a new order in Greater East Asia.

---

[1] Office of United States Chief of Counsel For Prosecution of Axis Criminality, *Nazi Conspiracy and Aggression* (Washington, 1946), vol. V, pp. 355-57.

Article 3

Germany, Italy, and Japan agree to cooperate in their efforts on the aforesaid basis. They further undertake to assist one another with all political, economic, and military means, if one of the Three Contracting Parties is attacked by a Power at present not involved in the European war or in the Chinese-Japanese conflict.

Article 4

For the purpose of implementing the present pacts, joint technical commissions, the members of which are to be appointed by the Governments of Germany, Italy, and Japan, will meet without delay.

Article 5

Germany, Italy, and Japan affirm that the aforesaid terms do not in any way affect the political status which exists at present between each of the three Contracting Parties and Soviet Russia.

Article 6

The present Pact shall come into force immediately upon signature and shall remain in force for ten years from the date of its coming into force.

At the proper time before expiration of the said term the High Contracting Parties shall, if one of them so requests, enter into negotiations for its renewal.

In faith whereof, the undersigned, duly authorized by their governments, have signed this pact and have hereunto apposed their seals.

Done in 3 original copies at Berlin, on the 27th day of September, 1940, in the XVIIIth year of the Fascist Era, corresponding to the 27th day of the 9th month of the 15th year of the Showa era.

Joachim von Ribbentrop
Ciano
[Signature of the Japanese Representative]

Document No. 2

IWAKURO-DROUGHT DRAFT PROPOSAL[2]

Submitted to the State Deparment on April 9, 1941, the Iwakuro-Drought Draft Proposal contained the principal demands of Japan upon the Unites States, points which remained at issue during the entire course of the Hull-Nomura conversations. Based on the suggestions of Bishop James E. Walsh and Father James M. Drought, it was drawn up by Colonel Hideo Iwakuro with the assistance of Father Drought as well as others.

γ   γ   γ

Proposal Presented to the Department of State Through the Medium of Private American and Japanese Individuals on April 9, 1941

The Governments of the United States and of Japan accept joint responsibility for the initiation and conclusion of a general agreement disposing the resumption of our traditional friendly relations.

Without reference to specific causes of recent estrangement, it is the sincere desire of both Governments that the incidents which led to the deterioration of amicable sentiment among our peoples should be prevented from recurrence and corrected in their unforseen and unfortunate consequences.

It is our present hope that, by a joint effort, our nations may establish a just Peace in the Pacific; and by the rapid consummation of an *entente cordiale,* arrest, if not dispel, the tragic confusion that now threatens to engulf civilization.

For such decisive action, protracted negotiations would seem ill-suited and weakening. We, therefore, suggest that adequate instrumentalities should be developed for the realization of a general agreement which would bind, meanwhile, both governments in honor and act.

[2] United States Department of State, *Papers Relating to the Foreign Relations of the United States; Japan, 1931-1941* (2 vols., Washington, 1943), vol. II, pp. 398-401.

It is our belief that such an understanding should comprise only the pivotal issues of urgency and not the accessory concerns which could be deliberated at a Conference and appropriately confirmed by our respective Governments.

We presume to anticipate that our Governments could achieve harmonious relations if certain situations and attitudes were clarified or improved; to wit:

1. The concepts of the United States and of Japan respecting international relations and the character of nations.
2. The attitudes of both governments toward the European War.
3. The relations of both nations toward the China affair.
4. Naval, aerial and mercantile marine relations in the Pacific.
5. Commerce between both nations and their financial cooperation.
6. Economic activity of both nations in the Southwestern Pacific area.
7. The policies of both nations affecting political stabilization in the Pacific.

Accordingly, we have come to the following mutual understanding subject, of course, to modifications by the United States Government and subject to the official and final decision of the Government of Japan.

I. The concepts of the United States and of Japan respecting national relations and the character of nations

The Governments of the United States and of Japan might jointly acknowledge each other as equally sovereign states and contiguous Pacific powers.

Both Governments assert the unanimity of their national policies as directed toward the foundation of a lasting peace and the inauguration of a new era of respectful confidence and cooperation among our peoples.

Both Governments might declare that is their traditional, and present, concept and conviction that nations

and races compose, as members of a family, one household; each equally enjoying rights and admitting responsibilities with a mutuality of interests regulated by powerful processes and directed to the pursuit of their moral
and physical welfare, which they are bound to defend for
themselves as they are bound not to destroy for others.

Both Governments are firmly determined that their
respective traditional concepts on the character of nations
and the underlying moral principles of social order and
national life will continue to be preserved and never trans-
formed by foreign ideas or ideologies contrary to those
moral principles and concepts.

II. The attitudes of both Governments toward the Euro-pean War.

The Government of Japan maintains that the purpose
of its Axis Alliance was, and is, defensive and designed to
prevent the extension of military grouping among nations
not directly affected by the European War.

The Government of Japan, with no intention of evad-
ing its existing treaty obligation, desires to declare that its
military obligation under the Axis Alliance comes into
force only when one of the parties of the Alliance is aggressively attacked by a power not at present involved in
the European War.

The Government of the United States maintains that
its attitude toward the European War is, and will continue
to be, determined by no aggressive alliance aimed to assist
any one nation against another. The United States maintains that it is pledged to the hate of war, and accordingly,
its attitude toward the European War is, and will continue
to be, determined solely and exclusively by considerations
of the protective defense of its own national welfare and
security.

III. China affairs.

The President of the United States, if the following
terms are approved by His Excellency and guaranteed by

the Government of Japan, might request the Chiang-Kai-Chek regime to negotiate peace with Japan.

    a. Independence of China
    b. Withdrawal of Japanese troops from Chinese territory, in accordance with an agreement to be reached between Japan and China.
    c. No acquisition of Chinese territory
    d. No imposition of indemnities
    e. Resumption of the "Open Door"; the interpretation and application of which shall be agreed upon at some future, convenient time between the United States and Japan
    f. Coalescence of the Governments of Chiang-Kai-Chek and of Wang-Ching-Wei
    g. No large-scale or concentrated immigration of Japanese into Chinese territory
    h. Recognition of Manchukuo.

With the acceptance by the Chiang-Kai-Chek regime of the aforementioned Presidential request, the Japanese Government shall commence direct peace negotiations with the newly coalesced Chinese Government, or constituent elements thereof.

The Government of Japan shall submit to the Chinese concrete terms of peace, within the limits of aforesaid general terms and along the line of neighborly friendship, joint defense against communistic activities and economic cooperation.

Should the Chiang-Kai-Check regime reject the request of President Roosevelt, the United States Government shall discontinue assistance to the Chinese.

IV. Naval, aerial and mercantile marine relations in the Pacific.

    a. As both the Americans and the Japanese are desirous of maintaining the peace in the Pacific, they shall not resort to such disposition of their naval forces and aerial forces as to menace each other. Detailed, concrete agreement thereof shall be left for determination at the proposed joint Conference.

b. At the conclusion of the projected Conference, each nation might despatch a courtesy naval squadron to visit the country of the other and signalize the new era of Peace in the Pacific.

c. With the first ray of hope for the settlement of China affairs, the Japanese Government will agree, if desired, to use their good offices to release for contract by Americans certain percentage of their total tonnage of merchant vessels, chiefly for the Pacific service, so soon as they can be released from their present commitments. The amount of such tonnage shall be determined at the Conference.

V. Commerce between both nations and their financial cooperation.

When official approbation to the present understanding has been given by both Governments, the United States and Japan shall assure each other to mutually supply such commodities as are respectively available or required by either of them. Both governments further consent to take necessary steps to the resumption of normal trade relations as formerly established under the Treaty of Navigation and Commerce between the United States and Japan. If a new commercial treaty is desired by both governments, it could be elaborated at the proposed conference and concluded in accordance with usual procedure.

For the advancement of economic cooperation between both nations, it is suggested that the United States extend to Japan a gold credit in amounts sufficient to foster trade and industrial development directed to the betterment of Far Eastern economic conditions and to the sustained economic cooperation of the Governments of the United States and of Japan.

VI. Economic activity of both nations in the Southwestern Pacific area.

On the pledged basis of guarantee that Japanese activities in the Southwestern Pacific area shall be carried on by peaceful means without resorting to arms, American cooperation and support shall be given in the production and procurement of natural resources (such as oil, rubber, tin, nickel) which Japan needs.

VII. The policies of both nations affecting political stabilization in the Pacific.

a. The Governments of the United States and of Japan will not acquiesce in the future transfer of territories or the relegation of existing States within the Far East and in the Southwestern Pacific area to any European Power.

b. The Governments of the United States and Japan jointly guarantee the independence of the Philippine Islands and will consider means to come to their assistance in the event of unprovoked aggression by any third Power.

c. The Government of Japan requests the friendly and diplomatic assistance of the Government of the United States for the removal of Hongkong and Singapore as doorways to further political encroachment by the British in the Far East.

d. Japanese Immigration to the United States and to the Southwestern Pacific area shall receive amicable consideration—on a basis of equality with other nationals and freedom from discrimination.

Conference.

a. It is suggested that a Conference between Delegates of the United States and of Japan be held at Honolulu and that this Conference be opened for the United States by President Roosevelt and for Japan by Prince Konoye. The delegates could number less than five each, exclusive of experts, clerks, etc.

b. There shall be no foreign observers at the Conference.

c. This Conference could be held as soon as possible (May 1941) after the present understanding has been reached.

d. The agenda of the Conference would not include a reconsideration of the present understanding but would direct its efforts to the specification of the prearranged agenda and drafting of instruments to effectuate the understanding. The precise agenda could be determined upon by mutual agreement between both governments.

Addendum.

The present understanding shall be kept as a confidential memorandum between the Governments of the United States and of Japan.

The scope, character and timing of the announcement of this understanding will be agreed upon by both Governments.

SECRETARY HULL'S ORAL STATEMENT OF JUNE 21, 1941[3]

Hull's Oral Statement of June 21, 1941, which he handed to Nomura together with an American revision of Japan's draft proposals, highlighted the main differences between the two countries and contained complaints against pro-Nazi officials in Tokyo. Because of Matsuoka's irritation, it was withdrawn on July 17.

γ   γ   γ

Oral Statement Handed by the Secretary of State to the Japanese Ambassador (Nomura) on June 21, 1941

The Secretary of State appreciates the earnest efforts which have been made by the Japanese Ambassador and his associates to bring about a better understanding between our two countries and to establish peace in the Pacific area. The Secretary of State appreciates also the frankness which has characterized their attitude throughout the conversations which have been held. This Government is no less desirous than the Japanese Ambassador to bring about better relations between our two countries and a situation of peace in the Pacific area, and in that spirit the Secretary of State has given careful study to every aspect of the Japanese proposal.

The Secretary of State has no reason to doubt that many Japanese leaders share the views of the Japanese Ambassador and his associates as indicated above and would support action toward achieving those high objectives. Unfortunately, accumulating evidence reaches this Government from sources all over the world, including reports from sources which over many years have demonstrated sincere good will toward Japan, that some Japanese leaders in influential official positions are definitely committed to a course which calls for support of Nazi Germany and its policies of conquest and that the only kind of understanding with the United States which they

[3]*Foreign Relations, Japan,* vol. II, pp. 485-86.

would endorse is one that would envisage Japan's fighting on the side of Hitler should the United States become involved in the European hostilities through carrying out its present policy of self-defense. The tenor of recent public statements gratuitously made by spokesmen of the Japanese Government emphasizing Japan's commitments and intentions under the Tripartite Alliance exemplify an attitude which cannot be ignored. So long as such leaders maintain this attitude in their official positions and apparently seek to influence public opinion in Japan in the direction indicated, is it not illusory to expect that adoption of a proposal such as the one under consideration offers a basis for achieving substantial results along the desired lines?

Another source of misgiving in the Japanese proposal relates to the desire of the Japanese Government to include in its terms for a peaceful settlement to be offered to the Chinese Government a provision which would permit the stationing of Japanese troops in certain areas in Inner Mongolia and North China as a measure of cooperation with China in resisting communistic activities. While this Government has given careful thought to the considerations which have prompted the Japanese Government to make such a proposal, and while this Government does not desire to enter into the merits of such a proposal, it feels that the liberal policies to which the United States is committed, as explained on numerous occasions to the Japanese Ambassador and his associates, would not permit this Government to associate itself with any course which appears to be inconsistent with these policies. Furthermore, although in matters affecting only this country there might be some latitude of decision as to the qualifying of rights, the matter under discussion affects the sovereign rights of a third country, and accordingly it is felt that this Government must be most scrupulous in dealing with such a matter.

The Secretary of State has therefore reluctantly come to the conclusion that this Government must await some clearer indication than has yet been given that the Japanese

Government as a whole desires to pursue courses of peace such as constitute the objectives of the proposed understanding. This Government sincerely hopes that the Japanese Government will manifest such an attitude.

NOTE: In order to bring the current discussions up to date as far as the American attitude is concerned, there is being handed the Japanese Ambassador separately a revision, bearing the date of June 21, of the document marked "Unofficial, Exploratory and without Commitment" which was handed the Japanese Ambassador on May 31.

IMPERIAL CONFERENCE OF JULY 2, 1941[4]

At the Imperial Conference of July 2, 1941, the Japanese government laid out its course of temporary peace with Great Britain and the United States. Determined to advance toward the south, the conferees agreed not to let any obstacles stand in their way. A summary of the main points was intercepted.

γ   γ   γ

An Outline of the Policy of the Imperial Government in View of Present Developments

(Decision reached at the Conference held in the Imperial Presence on July 2)

I. POLICY

1. The Imperial Government is determined to follow a policy which will result in the establishment of the Greater East Asia Co-Prosperity Sphere and world peace, no matter what international developments take place.

2. The Imperial Government will continue its effort to effect a settlement of the China Incident and seek to establish a solid basis for the security and preservation of the nation. This will involve an advance into the Southern Regions and, depending on future developments, a settlement of the Soviet Question as well.

3. The Imperial Government will carry out the above program no matter what obstacles may be encountered.

II. SUMMARY

1. Steps will be taken to bring pressure on the Chiang Regime from the Southern approaches in order to bring about its surrender. Whenever demanded by future developments the rights of a belligerent will be resorted to against Chungking and hostile concessions taken over.

---

[4] *Pearl Harbor Attack*, Hearings Before the Joint Committee on the Investigation of the Pearl Harbor Attack, 79th Congress, 1st Session (Washington, 1946), Part XX, pp. 4018-19.

2. In order to guarantee national security and preservation, the Imperial Government will continue all necessary diplomatic negotiations with reference to the southern regions and also carry out various other plans as may be necessary. In case the diplomatic negotiations break down, preparations for a war with England and America will also be carried forward. First of all, the plans which have been laid with reference to French Indo-China and Thai will be prosecuted with a view to consolidating our position in the southern territories.

In carrying out the plans outlined in the foregoing article, we will not be deterred by the possibility of being involved in a war with England and America.

3. Our attitude with reference to the German-Soviet War will be based on the spirit of the Tri-Partite Pact. However, we will not enter the conflict for some time but will steadily proceed with military preparations against the Soviet and decide our final attitude independently. At the same time, we will continue carefully correlated activities in the diplomatic field.

In case the German-Soviet War should develop to our advantage, we will make use of our military strength, settle the Soviet question and guarantee the safety of our northern borders.

(Pencilled Note: On this occasion the Army and Foreign Minister Matsuoka took a strong attitude toward the Soviet Union, and the Army began concentrating its armed forces in Manchoukuo. This resolution was drawn up to off-set the policies of the Army and the Foreign Minister.)

4. In carrying out the preceding article all plans, especially the use of armed forces, will be carried out in such a way as to place no serious obstacles in the path of our basic military preparations for a war with England and America.

5. In case all diplomatic means fail to prevent the entrance of America into the European War, we will proceed in harmony with our obligations under the Tri-Partite Pact. However, with reference to the time and method of employing our armed forces we will take independent action.

6. We will immediately turn our attention to placing the nation on a war basis and will take special measures to strengthen the defenses of the nation.

7. Concrete plans covering this program will be drawn up separately.

Document No. 5

IMPERIAL CONFERENCE OF SEPTEMBER 6, 1941[5]

In the Imperial Conference of September 6, 1941, the Japanese decided to go to war with the Western powers should negotiations fail. Because they never abandoned their resolve, this conference turned out to be of great importance.

γ   γ   γ

Plans for the Prosecution of the Policy of the Imperial Government

(Agenda for a council in the Imperial Presence)

In view of the increasingly critical situation, especially the aggressive plans being carried out by America, England, Holland and other countries, the situation in Soviet Russia and the Empire's latent potentialities, the Japanese Government will proceed as follows in carrying out its plans for the southern territories as laid in "An Outline of the Policy of the Imperial Government in View of Present Developments".

1. Determined not to be deterred by the possibility of being involved in a war with America (and England and Holland) in order to secure our national existence, we will proceed with war preparations so that they be completed approximately toward the end of October.

2. At the same time, we will endeavor by every possible diplomatic means to have our demands agreed to by America and England. Japan's minimum demands in these negotiations with America (and England), together with the Empire's maximum concessions are embodied in the attached document.

3. If by the early part of October there is not reasonable hope of having our demands agreed to in the diplomatic negotiations mentioned above, we will immediately make up our minds to get ready for war against America (and England and Holland).

[5]*Pearl Harbor Attack*, Part XX, pp. 4022-23.

Policies with reference to countries other than those in the southern territories will be carried out in harmony with the plans already laid. Special effort will be made to prevent America and Soviet Russia from forming a united front against Japan.

ANNEX DOCUMENT

A List of Japan's Minimum Demands and her Maximum Concession in her Negotiations with America and England

I. *Japan's Minimum Demands in her Negotiations with America (and England).*

1. America and England shall not intervene in or obstruct a settlement by Japan of the China incident.

(a) They will not interfere with Japan's plan to settle the China Incident in harmony with the Sino-Japanese Basic Agreement and the Japan-China-Manchoukuo Tri Partite Declaration.

(b) America and England will close the Burma Route and offer the Chiang Regime neither military, political nor economic assistance.

Note: The above do not run counter to Japan's previous declarations in the "N" plan for the settlement of the China Incident. In particular, the plan embodied in the new Sino-Japanese Agreement for the stationing of Japanese troops in the specified areas will be rigidly adhered to. However, the withdrawal of troops other than those mentioned above may be guaranteed in principle upon the settlement of the China Incident.

Commercial operations in China on the part of America and England may also be guaranteed, in so far as they are purely commercial.

2. America and England will take no action in the Far East which offers a threat to the defense of the Empire.

(a) America and England will not establish military bases in Thai, the Netherlands East Indies, China or Far Eastern Soviet Russia.

(b) Their Far Eastern military forces will not be increased over their present strength.

Note: Any demands for the liquidation of Japan's special relations with French Indo-China based on the Japanese-French Agreement will not be considered.

3. America and England will cooperate with Japan in her attempt to obtain needed raw materials.

(a) America and England will restore trade relations with Japan and furnish her with the raw materials she needs from the British and American territories in the Southwest Pacific.

(b) America and England will assist Japan to establish close economic relations with Thai and the Netherlands East Indies.

II. *Maximum Concessions by Japan.*

It is first understood that our minumum demands as listed under I above will be agreed to.

1. Japan will not use French Indo-China as a base for operating against any neighboring countries with the exception of China.

Note: In case any questions are asked concerning Japan's attitude towards Soviet Russia, the answer is to be that as long as Soviet Russia faithfully carries out the Neutrality Pact and does not violate the spirit of the agreement by, for instance, threatening Japan or Manchuria, Japan will not take any military action.

2. Japan is prepared to withdraw her troops from French Indo-China as soon as a just peace is established in the Far East.

3. Japan is prepared to guarantee the neutrality of the Philippine Islands.

RESIGNATION OF THE THIRD KONOYE CABINET[6]

The following excerpts from Prime Minister Fumimaro Konoye's Memoirs illustrate the background of the formation of the cabinet headed by Hideki Tojo which finally led Japan into war against the United States.

γ γ γ

The 3d Konoye Cabinet started off with the great mission of readjusting the Japanese-American relations. For this reason, the retirement of Foreign Minister Matsuoka was brought about and as only that was done, it can be said that all efforts were solely exerted toward the accomplishment of this great mission ever since the formation of the Cabinet. However, America's attitude was by no means definite. There were various opinions as to why her attitude was not definite, but the opinion of the War Minister was that since America's basic policy is to advance into Asia, the reason for America's indefinite attitude is fundamental and consequently she lacks sincerity even in her negotiation. However, we continued our negotiation with the view that a temporary compromise and conciliation may be possible in regard to the current situation, even if our basic traditional policies may have been different.

Recently the negotiation reached a state of temporary deadlock due to the occupation of French Indo-China by our troops, but as it became known that we wouldn't go any further, the situation eased somewhat and the negotiation was again resumed. Hence, a message was sent to President Roosevelt on August 28 proposing a conference. Nevertheless, since President Roosevelt, in reply to this stated that he was willing to hold a conference, but would like to have a general agreement reached in regard to the important matters, at least, as a premise, an Imperial

[6]International Military Tribunal for the Far East, Proceedings, Document 499, Prosecution, pp. 10,251-71.

Conference was held on September 6 to determine the basis of the counter-measure for this.

As a result of the Imperial Conference it was decided to direct all our efforts toward the diplomatic negotiation to the end, but to resolutely assume a war policy in the event no means for the conclusion of the negotiation is reached by early October.

Since there was a time limit of by early October, the negotiation was carried on hurriedly and as it didn't progress as expected, September passed and October came with the negotiation still not going smoothly. At about that time, the supreme command group became boisterous and stated that they will wait until October 15, but won't extend it beyond that. Therefore, I requested the assembly of the War Minister, the Foreign Minister, the Navy Minister and the President of the Planning Board at Ogigaiso for a final conference on October 12.

However, on the day before the conference, Chief Oka of the Naval Affairs Bureau came and in talking with him, he stated that with the exception of the Naval General Staff, the brains of the Navy don't want a Japanese-American war, but since the Navy, herself, can not say "she can't do it" in view of her approval of the decision of the Imperial Headquarters, the Navy Minister will propose to leave it in the hands of the Prime Minister at tomorrow's conference; so we would like you to decide on continuing the diplomatic negotiation.

Under such circumstances, this important conference was held at 2 p. m. on October 12 at Ogigaiso. When the Prime Minister in opening the conference, stated:

"At last, we have come to the stage where we must decide whether it is to be war or peace. In regard to this, let us first study whether there is any hope for a successful conclusion of the diplomatic negotiation.

"War Minister TOJO, expressing the Army's point of view stated:

" 'There is absolutely no hope for a successful conclusion of the diplomatic negotiation.' "

"However, Navy Minister OIKAWA stated:

" 'Let us leave the decision as to whether there is any hope for a successful conclusion of the diplomatic negotiation in the hands of the Prime Minister and the Foreign Minister and as for the Navy, she will comply with that decision. If there is any hope for a successful conclusion of the diplomatic negotiation, we want the negotiation to be continued. Today, we are standing on the cross-roads of peace or war. Until today, we have been making preparations for war on the one hand, while carrying on diplomatic negotiations on the other, but today we are actually confronting the crisis of peace or war. That is, if we are to rely on diplomatic negotiation, we would like it to be carried out thoroughly. Our preparations will fall behind if our attitude is to carry on diplomatic negotiation and then decide on war in the midst of it because it won't go smoothly. If we are to depend on diplomatic negotiation, we want to make it a success at all cost. Since we are standing on this important cross-road today, we want the decision of the Prime Minister at this time. We want to comply with this decision and go ahead.'

"Against this opinion of the Navy Minister, the War Minister replied:

" 'The Premier, of course, is shouldering a grave responsibility, but we, too, are responsible as advisers. Hence, the determination of this great problem cannot be left solely in the hands of the Premier. I believe that there is no hope for a successful conclusion of the diplomatic negotiation, but if the Foreign Minister is fully confident of success, it may be given further consideration. Does the Foreign Minister have a confidence of success?'

"Since Foreign Minister TOYODA's views were asked, the Foreign Minister stated:

" 'Since there is the second party, I can't say that I am confident of success, but, generally speaking, the important points in the negotiation with America are:

" '(1)   The Tripartite Alliance.

" '(2)   The economic problem in China.

" '(3)   The question of keeping our troops/T.N. in China/.

" 'These three items are the obstacles. Of these, some sort of agreement can be reached in regard to item 1 and 2, but the third item pertaining to the question of keeping our troops/T.N. in China/ is the most difficult one. Since America is emphatically demanding for the complete withdrawal of our troops, I believe a compromise may be reached if we agree to a complete withdrawal of troops as a principle and station troops according to the time and place as specifically designated by an agreement or something between Japan and China, but I believe even this will be considerably difficult.'

"When this opinion was expressed, the War Minister, objecting emphatically, stated:

" 'We can't yield on the question of withdrawal of troops. It must be done with occupation as its general principle and the remaining troops withdrawn. Since we have made such a tremendous sacrifice in this China Incident, it would be alright properly speaking, to sever her territory, but in view of the KONOYE statement, that, too, cannot be done. Besides, a complete withdrawal of troops now cannot be done.'

"Hence, the Prime Minister stated:

" 'If the War Minister insists, as he does, it is not a question of whether there is any hope for a successful conclusion of the diplomatic negotiation. There definitely is no hope. As for the Foreign Minister, he could consider it from the standpoint of the general situation and yield more. Only then, can it be said that there is hope for a successful conclusion of the negotiation. The Navy Minister is incessantly clamoring for the decision of the Premier, but I cannot decide on war at this time. Since I, as expressed in the opinion of the Foreign Minister, believe there is still hope of success, I cannot help but adopt the Foreign Minister's opinion if I must decide on one or the other.'

"At this point, the War Minister retorted:

" 'It is still early for the Premier to cast a decision. We would like to have him consider the matter once more.'

"As it was mutually decided to reconsider the matter, the conference of four and a half hours was brought to an end at 6:30 p.m. . . . .

"Therefore, at 8 o'clock on the night of the 15th, I secretly visited the residence of Prince HIGASHI-KUNI and informed him of the circumstances to date. And when I told him:

" 'In connection with our desire that the war must be prevented somehow, to solicit for the aid of an Imperial prince is an unprecedented thing, but there is no means other than this to return the decision of the past to a clean slate. The Lord Keeper of the Privy Seal KIDO is afraid that it may affect your reputation, but since it will bring trouble to not only Your Highness, but also to the Imperial Household if war should break out, I beg that you consider yourself to be Prince MORINAGA and put forth your whole effort at this time.'

His Imperial Highness stated that he would like to think it over since it was a grave matter and wondered if he could suppress the Army with his own strength.

"On the 16th, I began collecting the letters of resignation of the Cabinet Members from morning and when I informed the Lord Keeper of the Privy Seal KIDO that I was going to the palace to present them to the Emperor now as I had collected all of them in the afternoon, the Lord Keeper of the Privy Seal asked me to hold off. Stating that because I had collected all of the letters of resignation, I visited the palace at 5 o'clock and explaining the reason as disagreement of opinion within the Cabinet, I presented the resignation of the entire Cabinet Members and retired from the presence of the Emperor. I met the Lord Keeper of the Privy Seal KIDO and inquired as to what he thought of the Imperial prince. According to the Lord Keeper of the Privy Seal, since His Majesty claims that it would be very embarrassing, he has finally decided to summon both, TOJO and OIKAWA, simultaneously, issue the Imperial Mandate for the formation of the succeeding Cabinet to one of them and order the other to cooperate and, at the same time, he also issued an instruction to the effect that the decision of the Imperial Conference of September 6 be reconsidered.

"As to whom it shall be, the Lord Keeper of the Privy Seal explained that since the War Minister had clashed head-on with the Premier, it would be like recognizing his contention if it is given to him. Hence, he believes that it would be better to take the middle course and offer it to the Navy Minister — since the Navy Minister actually does not want war, but this has not been brought to light. The Emperor, too, has been informed to that effect.

"However, it can be thought in this maner, also. Since the problem is the Army, there would be a danger of the Army springing back all the more if it is offered to the Navy. Hence, wouldn't it be better to offer it to the stronger side and alleviate the situation? Since America is of the opinion that the Army would reverse things even if decided upon by the KONOYE Cabinet, she will be all the more surprised if TOJO Cabinet is formed after it, in view of the fact that she already is all the more convinced that it will be war with the resignation of the KONOYE Cabinet. But if the TOJO Cabinet, contrary to expectations, should continue to carry on the negotiation, it may instead make her feel relieved and bring about a better result. /TN: The following sentence is crossed out/ As to whom it should be, I believe that it would be better to have TOJO."

"Upon expressing my opinion thusly /TN: crossed out/, the Lord Keeper of the Privy Seal asked me to consider the above advantages and disadvantages until tommorrow.

"On the morning of the 17th, I sent a message to the Lord Keeper of the Privy Seal that TOJO would be better (if guarantee of peace is obtained).

"On the 17th, the chief retainers' conference will be held in the palace at 1 p.m., after which the Emperor is expected to summon both TOJO and OIKAWA and issue the Imperial Mandate and, at the same time, an instruction to the effect that the Army and the Navy should cooperate and that the decision of the Imperial Conference of September 6 should be reconsidered."

PROPOSAL "A"[7]

Proposals "A" and "B" constituted the Tojo govern-
ment's last offers to the United States. They were inter-
cepted by Magic, so that Secretary Hull and President
Roosevelt knew beforehand what to expect from Ambas-
sador Nomura. The following documents consist of Ad-
miral Nomura's note to the Secretary of State on Novem-
ber 7, as well as his remarks to the President three days
later, records together containing Proposal "A."

γ   γ   γ

Document Handed by the Japanese Ambassador (Nomura)
to the Secretary of State on November 7, 1941

(Tentative translation)

DISPOSITION OF JAPANESE FORCES

(A) Stationing of Japanese forces in China and the with-
drawal thereof:

With regard to the Japanese forces that have been despatched to China in connection with the China Affair,
those forces in specified areas in North China and Mengchiang (Inner Mongolia) as well as in Hainan-tao (Hainan
Island) will remain to be stationed for a certain required
duration after the restoration of peaceful relations betwen
Japan and China. All the rest of such forces will commence
withdrawal as soon as general peace is restored between
Japan and China, and the withdrawal will proceed according to separate arrangements between Japan and China
and will be completed within two years with the firm establishment of peace and order.

(B) Stationing of Japanese forces in French Indo-China
and the withdrawal thereof:

The Japanese Government undertakes to guarantee the
territorial sovereignty of French Indo-China. The Japanese

[7]*Foreign Relations, Japan: 1931-1941*, vol. II, pp. 709-10, 715-17.

forces at present stationed there will be withdrawn as soon as the China Affair is settled or an equitable peace is established in East Asia.

PRINCIPLE OF NON-DISCRIMINATION

The Japanese Government recognizes the principle of non-discrimination in international commercial relations to be applied to all the Pacific areas, inclusive of China, on the understanding that the principle in question is to be applied uniformly to the rest of the entire world as well.

Memorandum by the Secretary of State

[WASHINGTON,]   November 10, 1941.

The Japanese Ambassador, accompanied by Minister Wakasugi, called on the President. The Secretary of State was present at the express wish of President Roosevelt. The Ambassador, after a few preliminary remarks, proceeded to read as under instruction from his Government the following communication:

"I am not going to explain to you the salient points of the proposals which my Government has instructed me to submit to your Government. As you will recall, it was on the 25th of September that the Japanese Government, last made its proposals to the United States Government, and, gathering from the observations which the Secretary of State made on them on the 2nd of October and also from the views which are subsequently expressed by the Secretary of State and the Under-Secretary of State Mr. Welles, the greatest difficulties arose from three points, that is:—

1. The application of the principle of non-discrimination in international commercial relations.
2. The attitude of our two Governments toward the European war, and
3. The question of the stationing and withdrawal of Japanese forces.

"In regard to the first question, that is, the principle of non-discrimination, my Government has now decided to accept its application in all the Pacific areas, including China, as your Government desires, on the understanding that the principle is to be applied uniformly to the rest of the world as well. The Secretary of State has repeatedly pointed out to me that it has been his long-cherished scheme to see the application of the principle throughout the whole world. I therefore hope that the assurance to be given by my Government in this connection will be gratifying to you.

"As to the second question, the attitude of our two Governments toward the European war, my Government proposed, in the draft of September 25th, that

'both Governments will be guided in their conduct by considerations of protection and self-defense.'

In this connection I have to inquire if the United States Government is in a position to give an assurance that it has no intention of placing too liberal an interpretation on the term 'protection and self-defense' that may lead to an abuse of the recognized right based upon it. The Japanese Government would be ready to give a similar assurance on the basis of reciprocity, that is, if the assurance is forthcoming from the United States Government.

"In the draft of September 25th referred to, my Government proposed that

'in case the United States should participate in the European war, Japan would decide entirely independently in the matter of interpretation of the Tripartite Pact between Japan, Germany and Italy, and would likewise determine what actions might be taken by way of fulfilling the obligations in accordance with the said interpretation.'

It will hardly be necessary to point out in this connection that the fundamental motive for initiating the present conversations was the preservation of peace in the Pacific by all possible means. The present circumstances under which Japan is placed do not permit my Government to go any further to write in black and white than what it proposed in the draft of September 25th which I have just quoted. ~~All I have to ask you is to 'read between the lines' and to accept the formula as satisfactory.~~ (Deleted by Ambassador Nomura.) You will agree with me that where there is no mutual confidence and trust, a thousand words or letters would not be a satisfactory assurance.

"In regard to the third question, the stationing and withdrawal of Japanese forces, the formula which my Government wants to submit is as follows:

'With regard to the Japanese forces which have been despatched to China in connection with the China Affair, those forces in specified areas of North China and Mengchiang (Inner Mongolia) as well as in Hainan-tao (Hainan Island) will remain to be stationed for a certain required duration after the restoration of peaceful relations between Japan and China. All the rest of such forces will commence withdrawal as soon as general peace is restored between Japan and China and the withdrawal will proceed according to separate arrangements between Japan and China and will be completed within two years with the firm establishment of peace and order.'

"In submitting this formula, the Japanese Government has gone a great deal further than it went previously in that the formula specifies not only the areas in, but also the duration for, which the Japanese Government desires to have its forces remaining in China, clearly indicating that the stationing of the Japanese forces in China is not of a permanent nature. You will readily agree that, while complete and immediate withdrawal of all the Japanese forces from China may be desirable, it is impracticable under the present circumstances. I therefore earnestly hope that you will give favorable consideration from a practical standpoint.

"I have been instructed to add that, in regard to the Japanese forces in French Indo-China, the Japanese Government proposes the following formula:

"The Japanese Government undertake to respect the territorial sovereignty of French Indo-China. The Japanese forces at present stationed there will be withdrawn as soon as the China Affair is settled or an equitable peace is established in East Asia.' "[47]

The Ambassador then read the following manuscript which he said was an oral statement by him:

"I am very glad to be able to see you to-day, because since the resignation of the Cabinet of Prince Konoye, the conversations between the Secretary of State and myself had to be left alone for nearly three weeks—three weeks, even three days, are very precious time under the present circumstances. I am sure you will agree with me that the situation between Japan and the United States must not be left alone to take its own course and drift away beyond rescue.

"It is more than six months since the present informal conversations were started. From the very beginning the Japanese Government was very anxious to reach the earliest possible conclusion and the Japanese people placed a great deal of hope on it, but the conversations dragged on and on and, on the other hand, the relations between our two countries became more and more strained, the people of my country becoming more and more impatient.

"As viewed from the Japanese side, the Japanese Government has made not a few concession in its assertion at various stages while the United States Government has, it seemed to the Japanese, remained adamant on its contention and has shown little sign of reciprocation, and thus I must frankly inform you that in certain quarters in my country some skepticism has arisen as to the true intention of the United States Government. Personally I do not like to say it, but it is true. People in my country take the freezing of the assets as an economic blockade and they go even so far as to contend that the means of modern warfare are not limited to shooting. No nation can live without the supply of materials vital to its industries. Reports reaching me from home indicate that the situation

[47]The Japanese Ambassador also handed to President Roosevelt a copy of the document given the Secretary of State on November 7, 1941, p. 709. (See above).

is serious and pressing and the only way of preserving peace is to reach some kind of amicable and satisfactory understanding with the United States without any unnecessary loss of time. In the face of these mounting difficulties, the Japanese Government bent all its efforts to continue the conversations and bring about a satisfactory understanding solely for the purpose of maintaining peace in the Pacific. My Government therefore is now submitting certain proposals as its utmost effort for that purpose, and I shall feel very grateful if I can have the views of your Government on them at the earliest possible opportunity. Suppose we come to an understanding with this country, the psychological effect of it upon our people will mean much more than what is actually written upon the paper, and the policy of our Government will necessarily be guided and dictated thereby. I confidently hope that the views and desires entertained by the Japanese Government are fully shared and reciprocated by your Government.

"I may add for your information that in view of the serious situation now prevailing in the relations between our two countries, the Japanese Government is sending over here Ambassador Kurusu to assist me in the present conversations and also that the conversations will be taken up by Foreign Minister Togo with Ambassador Grew in Tokyo in a parallel line.

"I am afraid I may have used to-day some words which a trained diplomat must not use, but I hope you will kindly forgive my transgression, for it was only because of my earnest wish to keep and direct the relations of our two countries in the course which I believe is best for both of us."

The Ambassador appeared very much in earnest in reading the statement.

PROPOSAL "B"[8]

Proposal "B" represented the outer limit of Japan's concessions. In effect a modus vivendi, *it led to the brief consideration of an American couterproposal (See Document 9), which also attempted to establish a temporary solution.*

γ   γ   γ

Draft Proposal Handed by the Japanese Ambassador (Nomura) to the Secretary of State on November 20, 1941

1. Both the Governments of Japan and the United States undertake not to make any armed advancement into any of the regions in the South-eastern Asia and the Southern Pacific area excepting the part of French Indo-China where the Japanese troops are stationed at present.

2. The Japanese Government undertakes to withdraw its troops now stationed in French Indo-China upon either the restoration of peace between Japan and China or the establishment of an equitable peace in the Pacific area.

In the meantime the Government of Japan declares that it is prepared to remove its troops now stationed in the southern part of French Indo-China to the northern part of the said territory upon the conclusion of the present arrangement which shall later be embodied in the final agreement.

3. The Government of Japan and the United States shall cooperate with a view to securing the acquisition of those goods and commodities which the two countries need in Netherlands East Indies.

4. The Governments of Japan and the United States mutually undertake to restore their commercial relations to those prevailing prior to the freezing of the assets.

5. The Government of the United States undertakes to refrain from such measures and actions as will be prejudicial to the endeavors for the restoration of general peace between Japan and China.

[8]*Foreign Relations, Japan: 1931-1941*, vol. II, pp. 755-56

THE AMERICAN *MODUS VIVENDI* PROPOSAL[9]

The American proposal for a modus vivendi with Japan was briefly considered as a possible solution for the out-standing difficulties between the two countries. Always believed to be merely a short term answer, chiefly designed to gain three months' time, it was abandoned on November 26 when the Japanese were observed to be sending a convoy south from Shanghai and when the Chinese bitterly objected to it.

γ   γ   γ

Final Draft of Proposal "Modus Vivendi" With Japan[94]

[WASHINGTON,]   November 25, 1941.

The representatives of the Government of the United States and of the Government of Japan have been carrying on during the past several months informal and exploratory conversations for the purpose of arriving at a settlement if possible of questions relating to the entire Pacific area based upon the principles of peace, law and order and fair dealing among nations. These principles include the principle of inviolability of territorial integrity and sovereignty of each and all nations; the principle of equality, including equality of commerical opportunity and treatment; and the principle of reliance upon international cooperation and conciliation for the prevention and pacific settlement of controversies and for improvement of international conditions by peaceful methods and processes.

94. . . . On copy of this draft in FE Files, Lot 244, there appears a notation in red pencil by the Secretary of State as follows: "Final—Required final Conference with allied p[owe]rs before decision to use or not to by our Gov[ernment] — and therefore this paper was never presented to Japs. C[ordell] H[ull]".

[9] United States, Department of State, *Foreign Relations of the United States, Diplomatic Papers, 1941, Vol. IV, The Far East,* (Washington, 1956), pp. 661-64.

It is believed that in our discussions some progress has been made in reference to the general principles which constitute the basis of a peaceful settlement covering the entire Pacific area. Recently the Japanese Ambassador has stated that the Japanese Government is desirous of continuing the conversations directed toward a comprehensive and peaceful settlement in the Pacific area; that it would be helpful toward creating an atmosphere favorable to the successful outcome of the conversations if a temporary *modus vivendi* could be agreed upon to be in effect while the conversations looking to a peaceful settlement in the Pacific were continuing; and that it would be desirable that such *modus vivendi* include as one of its provisions some initial and temporary steps of a reciprocal character in the resumption of trade and normal intercourse between Japan and the United States.

On November 20 the Japanese Ambassador communicated to the Secretary of State proposals in regard to temporary measures to be taken respectively by the Government of Japan and by the Government of the United States, which measures are understood to have been designed to accomplish the purposes above indicated. These proposals contain features which, in the opinion of this Government, conflict with the fundamental principles which form a part of the general settlement under consideration and to which each Government has declared that it is committed.

The Government of the United Sates is earnestly desirous to contribute to the promotion and maintenance of peace in the Pacific area and to afford every opportunity for the continuance of discussions with the Japanese Government directed toward working out a broad-gauge program of peace throughout the Pacific area. With these ends in view, the Government of the United States offers for the consideration of the Japanese Government an alternative suggestion for a temporary *modus vivendi,* as follows:

MODUS VIVENDI

1. The Government of the United States and the Government of Japan, both being solicitous for the peace of the Pacific, affirm that their national policies are directed toward lasting and extensive peace throughout the Pacific area and that they have no territorial designs therein.

2. They undertake reciprocally not to make from regions in which they have military establishments any advance by force or threat of force into any areas in Southeastern or Northeastern Asia or in the southern or the northern Pacific area.

3. The Japanese Government undertakes forthwith to withdraw its armed forces now stationed in southern French Indochina and not to replace those forces; to reduce the total of its forces in French Indochina to the number there on July 26, 1941; and not to send additional naval, land or air forces to Indochina for replacements or otherwise.

The provisions of the foregoing paragraph are without prejudice to the position of the Government of the United States with regard to the presence of foreign troops in that area.

4. The Government of the United States undertakes forthwith to modify the application of its existing freezing and export restrictions to the extent necessary to permit the following resumption of trade between the United States and Japan in articles for the use and needs of their peoples:

(*a*) Imports from Japan to be freely permitted and the proceeds of the sale thereof to be paid into a clearing account to be used for the purchase of the exports from the United States listed below, and at Japan's option for the payment of interest and principal of Japanese obligations within the United States, provided that at least two-thirds in value of such imports per month consist of raw silk. It is understood that all American-owned goods now in Japan the movement of which in transit to the United States has been interrupted following the adoption of freezing measures shall be forwarded forthwith to the United States.

(*b*) Exports from the United States to Japan to be permitted as follows:

(i) Bunkers and supplies for vessels engaged in the trade here provided for and for such other vessels engaged in other trades as the two Governments may agree.

(ii) Food and food products from the United States subject to such limitations as the appropriate authorities may prescribe in respect of commodities in short supply in the United States.

(iii) Raw cotton from the United States to the extent of $600,000 in value per month.

(iv) Medical and pharmaceutical supplies subject to such limitations as the appropriate authorities may prescribe in respect of commodities in short supply in the United States.

(v) Petroleum. The United States will permit the export to Japan of petroleum, within the categories permitted general export, upon a monthly basis for civilian needs. The proportionate amount of petroleum to be exported from the United States for such needs will be determined after consultation with the British and the Dutch Governments. It is understood that by civilian needs in Japan is meant such purposes as the operation of the fishing industry, the transport system, lighting, heating, industrial and agricultural uses, and other civilian uses.

(vi) The above stated amounts of exports may be increased and additional commodities added by agreement between the two governments as it may appear to them that the operation of this agreement is furthering the peaceful and equitable solution of outstanding problems in the Pacific area.

5. The Government of Japan undertakes forthwith to modify the application of its existing freezing export restrictions to the extent necessary to permit the resumption

of trade between Japan and the United States as provided for in paragraph four above.

6. The Government of the United States undertakes forthwith to approach the Australian, British and Dutch Governments with a view to those Governments' taking measures similar to those provided for in paragraph four above.

7. With reference to the current hostilities between Japan and China, the fundamental interest of the Government of the United States in reference to any discussions which may be entered into between the Japanese and the Chinese Governments is simply that these discussions and any settlement reached as a result thereof be based upon and exemplify the fundamental principles of peace, law, order and justice, which constitute the central spirit of the current conversations between the Government of Japan and the Government of the United States and which are applicable uniformly throughhout the Pacific area.

8. This *modus vivendi* shall remain in force for a period of three months with the understanding that the two parties shall confer at the instance of either to ascertain whether the prospects of reaching a peaceful settlement covering the entire Pacific area justify an extension of the *modus vivendi* for a further period.

There is attached in tentative form a plan of a comprehensive peaceful settlement covering the entire Pacific area as one practical exemplificaton of the kind of program which this Government has in mind to be worked out during the further conversations between the Government of Japan and the Government of the United States while this *modus vivendi* would be in effect.

Document No. 10

THE TEN-POINT NOTE OF NOVEMBER 26, 1941[10]

The ten-point note which Secretary of State Hull handed to Ambassador Nomura on November 26, 1941, has been called an ultimatum. Preceded by an oral statement emphasizing America's desire for peace, it made no demands upon Japan which could be considered final propositions the refusal of which would lead to war. Nevertheless, its terms were so sweeping that its rejection was a virtual certainty.

γ   γ   γ

Document Handed by the Secretary of State to the Japanese Ambassador (Nomura) on November 26, 1941

Strictly Confidential,
Tentative and Without
Commitment.   **WASHINGTON**, November 26, 1941.

Outline of Proposed Basis for Agreement Between the United States and Japan

SECTION I

Draft Mutual Declaration of Policy

The Government of the United States and the Government of Japan both being solicitous for the peace of the Pacific affirm that their national policies are directed toward lasting and extensive peace throughout the Pacific area, that they have no territorial designs in that area, that they have no intention of threatening other countries or of using military force aggressively against any neighboring nation, and that, accordingly, in their national policies they will actively support and give practical application to the following fundamental principles upon which their relations with each other and with all other governments are based:

(1) The principle of inviolability of territorial integrity and sovereignty of each and all nations.

[10]*Foreign Relations, Japan: 1931-1941*, vol. II, pp. 768-70.

(2) The principle of non-interference in the internal affairs of other countries.

(3) The principle of equality, including equality of commercial opportunity and treatment.

(4) The principle of reliance upon international co-operation and conciliation for the prevention and pacific settlement of controversies and for improvement of international conditions by peaceful methods and processes.

The Government of Japan and the Government of the United States have agreed that toward eliminating chronic political instability, preventing recurrent economic collapse, and providing a basis for peace, they will actively support and practically apply the following principles in their economic relations with each other and with other nations and peoples:

(1) The principle of non-discrimination in international commercial relations.

(2) The principle of international economic cooperation and abolition of extreme nationalism as expressed in excessive trade restrictions.

(3) The principle of non-discriminatory access by all nations to raw material supplies.

(4) The principle of full protection of the interests of consuming countries and populations as regards the operation of international commodity agreements.

(5) The principle of establishment of such institutions and arrangements of international finance as may lend aid to the essential enterprises and the continuous development of all countries and may permit payments through processes of trade consonant with the welfare of all countries.

SECTION II

Steps To Be Taken by the Government of the United States and by the Government of Japan

The Government of the United States and the Government of Japan propose to take steps as follows:

1. The Government of the United States and the Government of Japan will endeavor to conclude a multilateral

non-aggression pact among the British Empire, China, Japan, the Netherlands, the Soviet Union, Thailand and the United States.

2. Both Governments will endeavor to conclude among the American, British, Chinese, Japanese, the Netherland and Thai Governments an agreement whereunder each of the Governments would pledge itself to respect the territorial integrity of French Indochina and, in the event that there should develop a threat to the territorial integrity of Indochina, to enter into immediate consultation with a view to taking such measures as may be deemed necessary and advisable to meet the threat in question. Such agreement would provide also that each of the Governments party to the agreement would not seek or accept preferential treatment in its trade or economic relations with Indochina and would use its influence to obtain for each of the signatories equality of treatment in trade and commerce with French Indochina.

3. The Government of Japan will withdraw all military, naval, air and police forces from China and from Indochina.

4. The Government of the United States and the Government of Japan will not support—militarily, politically, economically—any government or regime in China other than the National Government of the Republic of China with capital temporarily at Chungking.

5. Both Governments will give up all extraterritorial rights in China, including rights and interests in and with regard to international settlements and concessions, and rights under the Boxer Protocol of 1901.

Both Governments will endeavor to obtain the agreement of the British and other governments to give up extraterritorial rights in China, including rights in international settlements and in concessions and under the Boxer Protocol of 1901.

6. The Government of the United States and the Government of Japan will enter into negotiations for the conclusion between the United States and Japan of a trade agreement, based upon reciprocal most-favored-nation

treatment and reduction of trade barriers by both countries, including an undertaking by the United States to bind raw silk on the free list.

7. The Government of the United States and the Government of Japan will, respectively, remove the freezing restrictions on Japanese funds in the United States and on American funds in Japan.

8. Both Governments will agree upon a plan for the stabilization of the dollar-yen rate, with the allocation of funds adequate for this purpose, half to be supplied by Japan and half by the United States.

9. Both Governments will agree that no agreement which either has concluded with any third power or powers shall be interpreted by it in such a way as to conflict with the fundamental purpose of this agreement, the establishment and preservation of peace throughout the Pacific area.

10. Both Governments will use their influence to cause other governments to adhere to and to give practical application to the basic political and economic principles set forth in this agreement.

SECRETARY OF WAR HENRY L. STIMSON'S DIARY, NOVEMBER 25, 1941[11]

Secretary of War Stimson's diary for November 25, 1941, with its famous reference to the question of maneuvering the Japanese into firing the first shot, has been endlessly cited in works dealing with the Pearl Harbor controversy. The entry as published in the Congressional hearings follows.

γ   γ   γ

TUESDAY, NOVEMBER 25, 1941.

This was a very full day indeed. At 9:30 Knox and I met in Hull's office for our meeting of Three. Hull showed us the proposal for a 3 months' truce, which he was going to lay before the Japanese today or tomorrow. It adequately safeguarded all our interests, I thought as we read it, but I don't think there is any chance of the Japanese accepting it, because it was so drastic. In return for the propositions which they were to do; namely; to at once evacuate and at once to stop all preparations or threats of action, and to take no aggressive action against any of her neighbors, etc., we were to give them open trade in sufficient quantities only for their civilian population. This restriction was particularly applicable to oil. We had a long talk over the general situation.

Then at 12 o'clock we (viz, General Marshall and I) went to the White House, where we were until nearly half past one. At the meeting were Hull, Knox, Marshall, Stark, and myself. There the President, instead of bringing up the Victory Parade,[1] brought up entirely the relations with the Japanese. He brought up the event that we were likely to be attacked perhaps (as soon as) next Monday, for the Japanese are notorious for making an attack without

[11]*Pearl Harbor Attack*, Part XI, pp. 5433-34.
[1]This was an office nickname for the General Staff strategic plan of national action in case of war in Europe.

warning, and the question was what we should do. The
question was how we should maneuver them into the position of firing the first shot without allowing too much
danger to ourselves. It was a difficult proposition.[2] Hull
laid out his general broad propositions on which the thing
should be rested—the freedom of the seas and the fact
that Japan was in alliance with Hitler and was carrying out
his policy of world aggression. The others brought out the
fact that any such expedition to the South as the Japanese
were likely to take would be an encirclement of our interests in the Philippines and cutting into our vital supplies
of rubber from Malaysia. I pointed out to the President
that he had already taken the first steps towards an ultimatum in notifying Japan way back last summer that if
she crossed the border into Thailand she was violating our
safety and that therefore he had only to point out (to
Japan) that to follow any such expedition was a violation
of a warning we had already given. So Hull is to go to
work on preparing that. When I got back to the Department I found news from G-2 that an (a Japanese) expedition had started. Five divisions have come down from
Shantung and Shansi to Shanghai and there they had em-
barked on ships—30, 40, or 50 ships—and have been sighted
south of Formosa. I at once called up Hull and told him
about it and sent copies to him and to the President of
the message from G-2.

[2] Our military and naval advisers had warned us that we could not
safely allow the Japanese to move against British Malaysia or the
Dutch East Indies without attempting to prevent it.

PRESIDENTIAL ORDER TO CHARTER THREE SMALL VESSELS FOR A "DEFENSIVE IN- FORMATION PATROL"[12]

The Presidential directive to charter three small vessels for the purpose of a defensive information patrol in the South China Sea is one of the items revisionists have cited to prove Roosevelt's purpose to bring about an incident. The order was issued by the Chief of Naval Operations on December 2, 1941, and sent to Admiral Thomas C. Hart in Manila.

γ   γ   γ

Top Secret
2 December 1941
From: OPNAV
Action: CINCAF
Info:
012356

(Paraphrase)

President directs that the following be done as soon as possible and within two days if possible after receipt this despatch. Charter 3 small vessels to form a "defensive information patrol". Minimum requirements to establish identity as U.S. men-of-war are command by a naval officer and to mount a small gun and 1 machine gun would suffice. Filipino crews may be employed with minimum number of naval ratings to accomplish purpose which is to observe and report by radio Japanese movements in west China Sea and Gulf of Siam. One vessel to be stationed between Camranh Bay and Cape St. Jacques and one vessel off Pointe de Camau. Use of Isabel authorized by president as one of the three but not other naval vessels. Report measures taken to carry out presidents views. At same time inform me as to what reconnaissance measures are being regularly performed at sea by both army and navy whether by air surface vessels or submarines and your opinion as to the effectiveness of these measures.

[12]*Pearl Harbor Attack,* Part XIV, p. 1403.

Document No. 13

THE MERLE-SMITH MESSAGE[13]

The following telegram from the American military attaché in Melbourne, Australia, Colonel Van S. Merle-Smith, to the War Department and the Commanding General of the Hawaiian Department has been cited as alleged proof that the United States was obligated to join the British and Dutch in accordance with the war plans worked out during the staff conversations in 1941. General MacArthur in the Philippines also received a similar message. Plan A-2 was a joint British-Dutch-American-Canadian plan, and the unnamed government was that of Australia, which, for its own reasons, had held up the transmission of this message.

γ   γ   γ

December 7, 1941
7:58 P.M.
From Melbourne, Australia, via Honolulu.
To War Department and Commanding General Hawaiian Department.
Secret.
Number 24.   December 6th.

Based on Dutch intelligence report (unconfirmed here) of naval movements from Pelau objective Menado and/or Ambon, Dutch ordered execution plan A-2 and suggested RAAF reciprocal movement be directed Laha Ambon and Koepang. So ordered pm yesterday including flight Catalina to Rabaul task reconnaissance Buka and northwest passage Australian Army reinforcements Ambon Keopang subject to request Dutch East Indies. This message held 17 hours by . . . Government eight am. Dutch reported advancing planes to be on Keopang not now considered necessary. Eleven a m Chief of Air Corps desired proceed with all aircraft forward movements Manila informed.

MERLE SMITH.

[13]*Pearl Harbor Attack*, Part IX, p. 4566.

THE CREIGHTON TELEGRAM[14]

The telegram from Captain John M. Creighton, the American Naval Attaché at Singapore, to Admiral Hart, concerning Air Chief Marshal Sir Robert Brooke-Popham's information from London about assurance of American aid is one of the revisionists' alleged proofs of binding American commitments to Great Britain. It was sent at 3:26 p.m., December 6, 1941 (Greenwich time).

γ   γ   γ

Brooke Popham received Saturday from War Department London Quote "We have now received assurance of American armed support in cases as follows:

Afirm we are obliged execute our plans to forestall Japs landing Isthmus of Kra or take action in reply to Nips invasion any other part of Siam XX Baker if Dutch Indies are attacked and we go to their defense XX Cast if Japs attack us the British XX Therefore without reference to London put plan in action if first you have good info Jap expedition advancing with the apparent intention of landing in Kra second if the Nips violate any part of Thailand Para if NEI are attacked put into operation plans agreed upon between British and Dutch" Unquote.

---

[14]*Pearl Harbor Attack*, Part X, pp. 5082-83.

Document No. 15

THE WINANT TELEGRAMS OF DECEMBER 2 AND 6, 1941 [15]

The two telegrams from the American Ambassador in Great Britain, John G. Winant, to the Secretary of State which follow have been cited by revisionists to support their contention that Roosevelt had prior commitments to aid the British in case of a Japanese attack in Southeast Asia. The first one was dated December 2, 1941, received at 10:40 a.m.; the second, 7 p.m., December 6, and received at 3:05 p.m. Both were marked "TRIPLE PRIORITY AND MOST URGENT."

γ   γ   γ

1. Winant to Hull, December 2, 1941

British Admiralty reports that at 3 a.m. London time this morning two parties seen off Cambodia Point, sailing slowly westward toward Kra 14 hours distant in time. First party 25 transports, 6 cruisers, 10 destroyers. Second party 10 transports, 2 cruisers, 10 destroyers.

WINANT.

2. Winant to Hull, December 6, 1941

"Personal and secret for the Secretary."

My number 5918 December 6, 4 p.m.

Again from Cadogan.

Admiralty conference on information just forwarded. Cadogan attending. They were uncertain as to whether destination of parties is Kra or Bangkok. Latter would be reached before Monday.

Note a discrepancy in time reported by me and time reported in our naval dispatch, latter stating 3 a.m., Greenwich time, my dispatch as given me at 3 a.m., London time. Believe former correct.

British feel pressed for time in relation to guaranteeing support Thailand, fearing Japan might force them to invite invasion on pretext protection before British have

[15] *Pearl Harbor Attack*, Part II, pp. 493-94, Part XIV, pp. 1247-48.

opportunity to guarantee support but wanting to carry out President's wishes in message transmitted by Welles to Halifax.

Leaving to spend evening with Eden in order to go over with him your Number 5682, December 5, although I had previously pressed on him each of the points you outlined prior to reception your message with the exception of paragraph 7 which I agree is not clear and which I will clear up with him this evening. I want you to know that I had nothing to do with the insertion of the reference to I. L. O.

I am having lunch with the Prime Minister tomorrow at his usual place in the country and will be constantly in contact with the Embassy over private wires in case you wish to communicate with me.

PRESIDENT ROOSEVELT'S REACTION TO THE FIRST THIRTEEN PARTS OF THE JAPANESE FOURTEEN-PART NOTE PRECEDING THE PEARL HARBOR ATTACK [16]

The following excerpts from the testimony of Commander Lester Robert Schulz, in 1941 the assistant to the White House Naval Aide, Captain John R. Beardall, sheds light on Roosevelt's reaction to the delivery of the first thirteen parts of the Japanese fourteen-part note intercepted on December 6. Seth W. Richardson was acting as General Counsel to the Joint Committee on the Investigation of the Pearl Harbor Attack.

γ   γ   γ

Mr. RICHARDSON. Were you on duty at the White House in Admiral Beardall's office there on the night of December 6, 1941?

Commander SCHULZ. I was on duty in the White House. Admiral Beardall had no fixed office in the White House at that time. He conducted his business for the most part in the Navy Department in the Navy Building and I was given a small office in a corner of the mail room, a closed office, but it was not a place used by Admiral Beardall.

Mr. RICHARDSON. That was at the White House?

Commander SCHULZ. Yes, sir; it was.

Mr. RICHARDSON. Do you recall Captain Kramer coming to the White House on the evening of December 6 to deliver any papers?

Commander SCHULZ. Yes, sir; I do.

Mr. RICHARDSON. About what time did he come?

Commander SCHULZ. Between 9 and 10; I should say about 9:30.

Mr. RICHARDSON. In the evening?

[16] *Pearl Harbor Attack*, Part X, pp. 4660-63.

Commander SCHULZ. In the evening; yes, sir.

Mr. RICHARDSON. Who was there besides you?

Commander SCHULZ. No one else of the Navy.

Mr. RICHARDSON. To whom, if anyone, did Captain Kramer hand his papers?

Commander SCHULZ. He handed them to me. They were in a locked pouch.

Mr. RICHARDSON. Was that the customary way in which dispatches that were being delivered there were delivered?

Commander SCHULZ. Material of that category was so delivered.

Mr. RICHARDSON. What did you do with the locked pouch when it was handed to you?

Commander SCHULZ. I took it from the mail room, which is in the office building, over to the White House proper and obtained permission to go up on the second floor and took it to the President's study.

Mr. RICHARDSON. Did you go alone?

Commander SCHULZ. I was accompanied by someone from the usher's office and announced to the President. However, then I was alone.

Mr. RICHARDSON. But Captain Kramer did not go with you?

Commander SCHULZ. That is correct, sir.

Mr. RICHARDSON. How long from the time the papers were placed in your hands by Captain Kramer was it before you went to the President's study?

Commander SCHULZ. About 5 minutes, I would say.

Mr. RICHARDSON. Whom did you find in the study when you arrived there?

Commander SCHULZ. The President was there seated at his desk, and Mr. Hopkins was there.

Mr. RICHARDSON. That is Mr. Harry Hopkins?

Commander SCHULZ. Yes, sir; that is correct.

Mr. RICHARDSON. You knew him?

Commander SCHULZ. Yes, sir. I had met him the previous day.

Mr. RICHARDSON. And you knew the President?

Commander SCHULZ. Yes, sir.

Mr. RICHARDSON. Was the pouch still locked?

Commander SCHULZ. I had a key to the pouch. I do not recall just when I unlocked it. In all likelihood it was after I was in the study, however.

Mr. RICHARDSON. What did you do after you entered the study?

Commander SCHULZ. I was announced and I informed the President that I had the material which Captain Kramer had brought and I took it out of the pouch.

Mr. RICHARDSON. Did you make any further statement at the time with reference to the material, as to your having been told that it was important or not?

Commander SCHULZ. That I do not recall, sir, but I believe that the President was expecting it. As I recall, he was.

Mr. RICHARDSON. Why? What makes you believe that? Was there anything said, I mean, that would indicate that?

Commander SCHULZ. When Admiral Beardall instructed me to stay and meet Captain Kramer and receive the material, he told me of its important nature.

Mr. RICHARDSON. Now, wait just a moment there.

Commander SCHULZ. And my recollection was also that it was of such importance that the President expected to receive it.

Mr. RICHARDSON. Before Captain Kramer came did you have a talk with Admiral Beardall with reference to the possibility of papers being delivered in the immediate future?

Commander SCHULZ. Yes, sir; I did. That is why I stayed.

Mr. RICHARDSON. What did Admiral Beardall say to you?

Commander SCHULZ. He told me that during the evening Captain Kramer would bring up some magic material and that I was to take it and give it immediately to the

President and he gave me the key to the pouch so that I could take it out and deliver it.

Mr. RICHARDSON. That is the substance of your conversation with Admiral Beardall?

Commander SCHULZ. Yes, sir; that is right.

Mr. RICHARDSON. Well, now, when you presented the material to the President, was it in the pouch?

Commander SCHULZ. To the best of my recollection I took it out of the pouch and handed it to him. The papers were clipped together. There were perhaps 15 typewritten pages and they were fastened together in a sheaf and I took them out of the pouch and handed them to the President personally.

Mr. RICHARDSON. You know now what we mean when we talk about the first 13 parts of the 14-part message; you know what I am talking about?

Commander SCHULZ. Yes, sir.

Mr. RICHARDSON. Are you able to state now whether among the papers which were delivered to the President there were this 13 parts of what was eventually the 14-part message?

Commander SCHULZ. No, sir; I cannot. I did not read the message. I have only learned of its substance through information that has been divulged during this inquiry, from newspapers and so on.

Mr. RICHARDSON. All right. Now, what happened when you delivered these papers to the President? You remained there?

Commander SCHULZ. Yes, sir; I remained in the room.

Mr. RICHARDSON. What happened?

Commander SCHULZ. The President read the papers, which took perhaps 10 minutes. Then he handed them to Mr. Hopkins.

Mr. RICHARDSON. How far away from the President was Mr. Hopkins sitting?

Commander SCHULZ. He was standing up, pacing back and forth slowly, not more than 10 feet away.

Mr. RICHARDSON. Did the President read out loud when he was reading the papers?

Commander SCHULZ. I do not recall that he did.

Mr. RICHARDSON. All right. Now go ahead and give us in detail just what occurred there, if you please, Commander.

Commander SCHULZ. Mr. Hopkins then read the papers and handed them back to the President. The President then turned toward Mr. Hopkins and said in substance—I am not sure of the exact words, but in substance—"This means war." Mr. Hopkins agreed, and they discussed then, for perhaps 5 minutes, the situation of the Japanese forces, that is, their deployment and—

Mr. RICHARDSON. Can you recall what either of them said?

Commander SCHULZ. In substance I can. There are only a few words that I can definitely say I am sure of, but the substance of it was that—I believe Mr. Hopkins mentioned it first—that since war was imminent, that the Japanese intended to strike when they were ready, at a moment when all was most opportune for them—

The CHAIRMAN. When all was what?

Commander SCHULZ. When all was most opportune for them. That is, when their forces were most properly deployed for their advantage. Indochina in particular was mentioned, because the Japanese forces had already landed there and there were implications of where they should move next.

The President mentioned a message that he had sent to the Japanese Emperor concerning the presence of Japanese troops in Indochina, in effect requesting their withdrawal.

Mr. Hopkins then expressed a view that since war was undoubtedly going to come at the convenience of the Japanese, it was too bad that we could not strike the first blow and prevent any sort of surprise. The President nodded and then said, in effect, "No we can't do that. We are a democracy and a peaceful people." Then he raised his voice, and this much I remember definitely. He said, "But we have a good record."

The impression that I got was that we would have to stand on that record, we could not make the first overt move. We would have to wait until it came.

During this discussion there was no mention of Pearl Harbor. The only geographic name I recall was Indochina. The time at which war might begin was not discussed, but from the manner of the discussion there was no indication that tomorrow was necessarily the day. I carried that impression away because it contributed to my personal surprise when the news did come.

Mr. RICHARDSON. Was there anything said, Commander, with reference to the subject of notice or notification as a result of the papers that were being read?

Commander SCHULZ. There was no mention made of sending any further warning or alert. However, having concluded this discussion about the war going to begin at the Japanese convenience, then the President said that he believed he would talk to Admiral Stark. He started to get Admiral Stark on the telephone. It was then determined—I do not recall exactly, but I believe the White House operator told the President that Admiral Stark could be reached at the National Theater.

Mr. RICHARDSON. Now, was it from what was said there that you draw the conclusion that that was what the White House operator reported?

Commander SCHULZ. Yes, sir. I did not hear what the operator said, but the National Theater was mentioned in my presence, and the President went on to state, in substance, that he would reach the admiral later, that he did not want to cause public alarm by having the admiral paged or otherwise when in the theater, where, I believe, the fact that he had a box reserved was mentioned and that if he left suddenly he would surely have been seen because of the position which he held and undue alarm might be caused, and the President did not wish that to happen because he could get him within perhaps another half an hour in any case.

Mr. RICHARDSON. Was there anything said about telephoning anybody else except Stark?

Commander SCHULZ. No sir; there was not.

THE "BOMB PLOT" MESSAGE[17]

The following message from Tokyo to the Japanese consulate in Honolulu has been called the "bomb plot." Because similar requests about other strategically vital areas were also intercepted, it was not considered a "bomb plot" at the time.

γ   γ   γ

From: Tokyo (Toyoda)
To: Honolulu
September 24, 1941
J-19
#83

Strictly secret.

Henceforth, we would like to have you make reports concerning vessels along the following lines insofar as possible:

1. The waters (of Pearl Harbor) are to be divided roughly into five sub-areas. (We have no objections to your abreviating as much as you like.)

Area A. Waters between Ford Island and the Arsenal.

Area B. Waters adjacent to the Island south and west of Ford Island. (This area is on the opposite side of the Island from Area A.)

Area C. East Loch.

Area D. Middle Loch.

Area E. West Loch and the communicating water routes.

2. With regard to warships and aircraft carriers, we would like to have you report on those at anchor, (these are not so important) tied up at wharves, buoys and in docks. (Designate types and classes briefly. If possible we would like to have you make mention of the fact when there are two or more vessels along side the same wharf.)

ARMY 23260   Trans. 10/9/41   (S)

---

[17]*Pearl Harbor Attack*, Part XII, p. 261.

SHIPS-IN-HARBOR MESSAGES[18]

The following messages constitute good examples of the detailed information sought by the Japanese about American ships at Pearl Harbor. Properly evaluated, they might have yielded important clues, but some were not available until after the Pearl Harbor attack.

γ γ γ

From: Tokyo (Togo)
To: Honolulu (Riyoji)
15 November 1941
(J19)
#111

As relations between Japan and the United States are most critical, make your "ships in harbor report" irregular, but at a rate of twice a week. Although you already are no doubt aware, please take extra care to maintain secrecy.
JD–1: 6991 25644   (Y) Navy Trans. 12–3–41   (S)

FROM: Tokyo (Togo)   November 28, 1941
TO: Honolulu   #119.

Re your message #243[a].

Secret outside the Department.

Intelligences of this kind which are of major importance, please transmit to us in the following manner:

1. When battleships move out of the harbor if we report such movement but once a week the vessels, in that interval, could not only be in the vicinity of the Hawaiian Islands, but could also have traveled far. Use your own judgment in deciding on reports covering such movements.

---

[18] *Pearl Harbor Attack,* Part XII, pp. 262, 266; Department of Defense, *The Magic Background of Pearl Harbor* (5 vols, Washington, 1977). vol. IV, app. A, 149-51.
[a] Not available.

2. Report upon the entrance or departure of capital ships and the length of time they remain at anchor, from the time of entry into the port until the departure.

Trans. 12–8–41

FROM: Tokyo   November 29, 1941
TO: Honolulu   #122.

We have been receiving reports from you on ship movements, but in future will you also report even when there are no movements.

Trans. 12–5–41

FROM: Tokyo (Togo)   December 2, 1941
TO: Honolulu   #123.

(Secret outside the department.)

In view of the present situation, the presence in port of warships, airplane carriers, and cruisers is of utmost importance. Hereafter, to the utmost of your ability, let me know day by day. Wire me in each case whether or not there are any observation balloons above Pearl Harbor or if there are any indications that they will be sent up. Also advise me whether or not the warships are provided with anti-mine nets.

Trans. 12–30–41

DEADLINE MESSAGES[19]

The following messages from the Tokyo Foreign Office to the Japanese Ambassador in Washington indicating that the Tojo government had set a deadline for the conclusion of the negotiations were duly intercepted in the United States. The Armed Forces' failure to forward them to Hawaii has been critized by the revisionists.

γ　　　　　γ　　　　　γ

[Secret]

From: Tokyo (Togo)
To:　Washington
November 2, 1941
Purple (CA)
#722

The Government has for a number of days since the forming of the new Cabinet been holding meetings with the Imperial headquarters. We have carefully considered a fundamental policy for improving relations between Japan and America, but we expect to reach a final decision in a meeting on the morning of the 5th and will let you know the result at once. This will be our Government's last effort to improve diplomatic relations. The situation is very grave. When we resume negotiations, the situation makes it urgent that we reach a decision at once. This is at present only for your information. When we take up these negotiations once more, we trust you will handle everything with the greatest of care.

Army 24292　　　　　　　　　Trans. 11–3–41　(S)

[Secret]

From:　Tokyo
To:　Washington
November 4, 1941
Purple (CA)　(Urgent)
#725　(Part 1 of 3)

[19]*Pearl Harbor Attack,* Part XII, pp. 90, 92-93, 100.

Concerning my #722[a].

1. Well, relations between Japan and the United States have reached the edge, and our people are losing confidence in the possibility of ever adjusting them. In order to lucubrate on a fundamental national policy, the Cabinet has been meeting with the Imperial Headquarters for some days in succession. Conference has followed conference, and now we are at length able to bring forth a counter-proposal for the resumption of Japanese-American negotiations based upon the unanimous opinion of the Government and the military high command (ensuing Nos. 726[b] and 727[b]). This and other basic policies of our Empire await the sanction of the conference to be held on the morning of the 5th.

2. Conditions both within and without our Empire are so tense that no longer is procrastination possible, yet in our sincerity to maintain pacific relationships between the Empire of Japan and the United States of America, we have decided, as a result of these deliberations, to gamble once more on the continuance of the parleys, but this is our last effort. Both in name and spirit this counter-proposal of ours is, indeed, the last. I want you to know that. If through it we do not reach a quick accord, I am sorry to say the talks will certainly be ruptured. Then, indeed, will relations between our two nations be on the brink of chaos. I mean that the success or failure of the pending discussions will have an immense effect on the destiny of the Empire of Japan. In fact, we gambled the fate of our land on the throw of this die.

Army 24330   Trans. 11/4/41 (S)
JD 6248

---

[a]S.I.S. #24292 which states that meetings are being held with the Imperial Headquarters to consider a fundamental policy for improving relations between Japan and America and that a final decision is to be made on the morning of the 5th.
[b]Not available.

From: Tokyo
To: Washington
November 4, 1941
Purple (CA) (Urgent)
#725 (Part 2 of 3)

When the Japanese-American meetings began, who
would have ever dreamt that they would drag out so
long? Hoping that we could fast come to some understanding, we have already gone far out of our way and
yielded and yielded. The United States does not appreci-
ate this, but through thick and thin sticks to the self-same
propositions she made to start with. Those of our people
and of our officials who suspect the sincerity of the Americans are far from few. Bearing all kinds of humiliating
things, our Government has repeatedly stated its sincerity
and gone far, yes, too far, in giving in to them. There is
just one reason why we do this—to maintain peace in the
Pacific. There seem to be some Americans who think we
would make a one-sided deal, but our temperance, I can
tell you, has not come from weakness and naturally there
is an end to our long-suffering. Nay, when it comes to a
question of our existence and our honor, when the time
comes we will defend them without recking the cost. If
the United States takes an attitude that overlooks or
shuns this position of ours, there is not a whit of use in
ever broaching the talks. This time we are showing the
limit of our friendship; this time we are making our last
possible bargain, and I hope that we can thus settle all
our troubles with the United States peaceably.

Army 24331   Trans. 11:4:41 (S)

[Part 3 omitted]

[Secret]

From: Tokyo
To: Washington
5 November 1941
(Purple—CA)
#736

(Of utmost secrecy).

Because of various circumstances, it is absolutely

necessary that all arrangements for the signing of this agreement be completed by the 25th of this month. I realize that this is a difficult order, but under the circumstances it is an unavoidable one. Please understand this thoroughly and tackle the problem of saving the Japanese-U.S. relations from falling into a chaotic condition. Do so with great determination and with unstinted effort, I beg of you.

This information is to be kept strictly to yourself only.

24373

JD–1: 6254   (D) Navy Trans. 11–5–41 (S–TT)

Document No. 20

ADDITIONAL DEADLINE MESSAGES AND EXTENSION OF THE DEADLINE [20]

The following messages indicate the urgency with which the Tokyo government regarded the need for an agreement. The extension of the deadline on November 22 merely emphasized this point.

γ   γ   γ

[Secret]

From: Tokyo
To: Washington
November 16, 1941
Purple (CA) (Urgent)
#———

For your Honor's own information.

1. I have read your #1090[a], and you may be sure that you have my gratitude for the efforts you have put forth, but the fate of our Empire hangs by the slender thread of a few days, so please fight harder than you ever did before.

2. What you say in the last paragraph of your message is, of course, so and I have given it already the fullest consideration, but I have only to refer you to the fundamental policy laid down in my #725.[b] Will you please try to realize what that means. In your opinion we ought to wait and see what turn the war takes and remain patient. However, I am awfully sorry to say that the situation renders this out of the question. I set the deadline for the solution of these negotiations in my #736,[c] and there will be no

---

[a]For Part 1, see S.I.S.#24877. For Part 2, see S.I.S. #24857 in which NOMURA gives his views on the general situation. Part 3 not available.

[b]S.I.S. #24330 in which TOGO says that conditions both within and without the Japanese Empire will not permit any further delay in reaching a settlement with the United States.

[c]S.I.S. #24373 in which TOGO says that is absolutely necessary that all arrangements for the signing of this agreement be completed by the 25th of this month.

[20]*Pearl Harbor Attack*, Part XII, 137-38, 165.

change. Please try to understand that. You see how short
the time is; therefore, do not allow the United States to
sidetrack us and delay the negotiations any further. Press
them for a solution on the basis of our proposals, and do
your best to bring about an immediate solution.

Army 24878   Trans. 11/17/41 (S)

[Secret]

From: Tokyo
To: Washington
November 22, 1941
Purple CA (Urgent)
#812

To both you Ambassadors.

It is awfully hard for us to consider changing the date
we set in my #736[a]. You should know this, however, I
know you are working hard. Stick to our fixed policy and
do your very best. Spare no efforts and try to bring about
the solution we desire. There are reasons beyond your
ability to guess why we wanted to settle Japanese-American
relations by the 25th, but if within the next three or four
days you can finish your conversations with the Americans; if the signing can be completed by the 29th, (let me
write it out for you—twenty ninth); if the pertinent notes
can be exchanged; if we can get an understanding with
Great Britain and the Netherlands; and in short if everything can be finished, we have decided to wait until that
date. This time we mean it, that the deadline absolutely
cannot be changed. After that things are automatically
going to happen. Please take this into your careful consideration and work harder than you ever have before. This,
for the present, is for the information of you two Ambassadors alone.

Army 25138   Trans. 11/22/41 (s)

[a]See S.I.S. #24373. Tokyo wires Washington that because of the
various circumstances it is absolutely necessary that arrangements for the signing of the agreement be completed by the
25th of this month.

Document No. 21

JAPANESE INSTRUCTIONS TO AMBASSADORS NOMURA AND KURUSU ABOUT BREAKING OFF NEGOTIATIONS [21]

The following message from Tokyo to the Japanese embassy in Washington was a clear sign of the Tojo government's determination to end the diplomatic talks. The unnamed person mentioned was the Navy Minister who was no longer interested in a diplomatic solution.

γ γ γ

[Secret]

From: Tokyo
To: Washington
November 28, 1941.
Purple (CA)
#844

Re your #1189

Well, you two Ambassadors have exerted superhuman efforts but, in spite of this, the United States has gone ahead and presented this humiliating proposal. This was quite unexpected and extremely regrettable. The Imperial Government can by no means use it as a basis for negotiations. Therefore, with a report of the views of the Imperial Government on this American proposal which I will send you in two or three days, the negotiations will be de facto ruptured. This is inevitable. However, I do not wish you to give the impression that the negotiations are broken off. Merely say to them that you are awaiting instructions and that, although the opinions of your Government are not yet clear to you, to your own way of thinking the Imperial Government has always made just claims and has borne great sacrifices for the sake of peace in the Pacific. Say that we have always demonstrated a long-suffering and conciliatory attitude, but that, on the other hand, the United States has been unbending, making it impossible for Japan to establish negotiations. Since things have come to this pass, I contacted the man you told me to in your #1180 and he said that under the present circumstances what you suggest is entirely unsuitable. From now on do the best you can.

Army 25445
JD 6898   Trans. 11–28–41 (S)

[21] *Pearl Harbor Attack,* Part XII, p. 195.

THE WINDS AND HIDDEN WORDS CODES[22]

The Winds and Hidden Words codes were set up on November 19, 1941. Whether a Winds-Execute message was ever received in Washington prior to Pearl Harbor has become one of the most persistent subjects of the controversy about the disaster.

γ   γ   γ

From: Tokyo
To: Washington
19 November 1941
(J 19)
Circular #2353

Regarding the broadcast of a special message in an emergency.

In case of emergency (danger of cutting off our diplomatic relations), and the cutting off of international communications, the following warning will be added in the middle of the daily Japanese language short wave news broadcast.

(1) In case of a Japan-U.S. relations in danger: HIGASHI NO KAZEAME.*

(2) Japan-U. S. S. R. relations: KITANOKAZE KUMORI.**

(3) Japan-British relations: NISHI NO KAZE HARE.***

This signal will be given in the middle and at the end as a weather forecast and each sentence will be repeated twice. When this is heard please destroy all code papers, etc. This is as yet to be a completely secret arrangement.

Forward as urgent intelligence.

25432
JD–1: 6875   (Y) Navy Trans. 11–28–41 (S–TT)

---

*East wind rain.
**North wind cloudy.
***West wind clear.
[22] *Pearl Harbor Attack,* Part XII, pp. 154, 155.

[Secret]

From: Tokyo
To: Washington
19 November 1941
(J19)
Circular #2354

When our diplomatic relations are becoming dangerous, we will add the following at the beginning and end of our general intelligence broadcasts:

(1) If it is Japan-U.S. relations, "HIGASHI".

(2) Japan-Russia relations, "KITA".

(3) Japan-British relations, (including Thai, Malaya and N.E.I.); "NISHI".

The above will be repeated five times and included at beginning and end.

Relay to Rio de Janeiro, Buenos Aires, Mexico City, San Francisco.

25392
JD–1: 6850   (Y) Navy Trans. 11–26–41 (S)

THE FOURTEEN-PART AND RELATED MESSAGES[23]

The following intercepts consist of the pilot message announcing the imminent transmittal of the Japanese reply to Hull's ten-point note, the fourteen-part message, instructions not to use typists, and the instructions for delivery of the document at 1:00 p.m. The pilot message and accompanying directives as well as the first thirteen parts of the fourteen-part note were received on December 6; the 1:00 p.m. note and the fourteenth part, on December 7, 1941.

γ   γ   γ

[Secret]

From: Tokyo
To: Washington
December 6, 1941
Purple
#901

Re my #844[a].

1. The Government has deliberated deeply on the American proposal of the 26th of November and as a result we have drawn up a memorandum for the United States contained in my separate message #902[b] (in English).

2. This separate message is a very long one. I will send it in fourteen parts and I imagine you will receive it tomorrow. However, I am not sure. The situation is extremely delicate, and when you receive it I want you to please keep it secret for the time being.

---

[a]See S.I.S. #25445 in which Tokyo wires Washington the Imperial government cannot accept the United States proposal and, therefore, with a report of the views of the Imperial Government will be sent in two or three days, the negotiations will be de facto ruptured. Until then, however, Washington is not to give the impression that negotiations are broken off.
[b]Not available.
[23]*Pearl Harbor Attack*, Part XII, pp. 238-45, 248.

3. Concerning the time of presenting this memorandum to the United States, I will wire you in a separate message. However, I want you in the meantime to put it in nicely drafted form and make every preparation to present it to the Americans just as soon as you receive instructions.

Army 25838
JD: 7149   Trans. 12–6–41 (S)

[Secret]

From: Tokyo
To: Washington
December 6, 1941
Purple
#902 (Part 1 of 14) Separate telegram

MEMORANDUM

1. The Government of Japan, prompted by a genuine desire to come to an amicable understanding with the Government of the United States in order that the two countries by their joint efforts may secure the peace of the Pacific area and thereby contribute toward the realization of world peace, has continued negotiations with the utmost sincerity since April last with the Government of the United States regarding the adjustment and advancement of Japanese-American relations and the stabilization of the Pacific area.

The Japanese Government has the honor to state frankly its views, concerning the claims the American Government has persistently maintained as well as the measures the United States and Great Britain have taken toward Japan during these eight months.

2. It is the immutable policy of the Japanese Government to insure the stability of East Asia and to promote world peace, and thereby to enable all nations to find each its proper place in the world.

Ever since the China Affair broke out owing to the failure on the part of China to comprehend Japan's true intentions, the Japanese Government has striven for the restoration of peace and it has consistently exerted its best efforts to prevent the extention of war-like disturbances. It was also to that end that in September last year Japan concluded the Tri Partite Pact with Germany and Italy. JD-1: 7143

25843   Navy Trans. 12-6-41 (S)

From: Tokyo
To: Washington
December 6, 1941
Purple
#902 (Part 2 of 14)

However, both the United States and Great Britain have resorted to every possible measure to assist the Chungking regime so as to obstruct the establishment of a general peace between Japan and China, interfering with Japan's constructive endeavours toward the stabilization of East Asia, exerting pressure on The Netherlands East Indies, or menacing French Indo-China, they have attempted to frustrate Japan's aspiration to realize the ideal of common prosperity in cooperation with these regions. Furthermore, when Japan in accordance with its protocol with France took measures of joint defense of French Indo-China, both American and British governments, wilfully misinterpreted it as a threat to their own possession and inducing the Netherlands government to follow suit, they enforced the assets freezing order, thus severing economic relations with Japan. While manifesting thus an obviously hostile attitude, these countries have strenghened their military preparations perfecting an encirclement of Japan, and have brought about a situation which endangers the very existence of the empire.

JD-1:7143   Navy Trans. 12-6-41 (S)
25843

From: Tokyo
To: Washington
December 6, 1941
Purple
#902 (Part 3 of 14)

Nevertheless, facilitate a speedy settlement, the Premier of Japan proposed, in August last, to meet the President of the United States for a discussion of important problems between the two countries covering the entire Pacific area. However, while accepting in principle the Japanese proposal, insisted that the meeting should take place after an agreement of view had been reached on fundamental—(75 letters garbled)— The Japanese government submitted a proposal based on the formula proposed by the American government, taking fully into consideration past American claims and also incorporating Japanese views. Repeated discussions proved of no avail in producing readily an agreement of view. The present cabinet, therefore, submitted a revised proposal, moderating still further the Japanese claims regarding the principal points of difficulty in the negotiation and endeavoured strenuously to reach a settlement. But the American government, adhering steadfastly to its original proposal, failed to display in the slightest degree a spirit of conciliation. The negotiation made no progress.

JD—1:7143   Navy Trans. 12-6-41 (S)
25843

From: Tokyo
To: Washington
December 6, 1941
Purple
#902 (Part 4 of 14)

Thereupon, the Japanese Government, with a view to doing its utmost for averting a crisis in Japanese-American relations, submitted on November 20th still another proposal in order to arrive at an equitable solution of the more essential and urgent questions which, simplifying its previous proposal, stipulated the following points:

(1) The Governments of Japan and the United States undertake not to dispatch armed forces into any of the regions, excepting French Indo-China, in the Southeastern Asia and the Southern Pacific area.

(2) Both Governments shall cooperate with a view to securing the acquisition in the Netherlands East Indies

of those goods and commodities of which the two countries are in need.

(3) Both Governments mutually undertake to restore commercial relations to those prevailing prior to the freezing of assets.

The Government of the United States shall supply Japan the required quantity of oil.

(4) The Government of the United States undertakes not to resort to measures and actions prejudicial to the endeavours for the restoration of general peace between Japan and China.

(5) The Japanese Government undertakes to withdraw troops now stationed in French Indo-China upon either the restoration of peace between Japan and China or the establishment of an equitable peace in the Pacific area; and it is prepared to remove the Japanese troops in the southern part of French Indo-China to the northern part upon the conclusion of the present agreement.

JD—17143   Navy Trans. 12-6-41 (S)
25843

[Secret]

From: Tokyo
To: Washington
December 6, 1941
Purple

#902 (Part 5 of 14)

As regards China, the Japanese Government, while expressing its readiness to accept the offer of the President of the United States to act as "Introducer" of peace between Japan and China as was previously suggested, asked for an undertaking on the part of the United States to do nothing prejudicial to the restoration of Sino-Japanese peace when the two parties have commenced direct negotiations.

The American government not only rejected the above-mentioned new proposal, but made known its intention to continue its aid to Chiang Kai-Shek; and in spite of its suggestion mentioned above, withdrew the offer of the

President to act as the so-called "introducer" of peace between Japan and China, pleading that time was not yet ripe for it. Finally, on November 26th, in an attitude to impose upon the Japanese government those principles it has persistently maintained, the American government made a proposal totally ignoring Japanese claims, which is a source of profound regret to the Japanese Government.

JD–1:7143   Navy Trans. 12-6-41 (S)
25843

[Secret]

From: Tokyo
To: Washington
December 6, 1941
Purple
#902 (Part 6 of 14)

4. From the beginning of the present negotiation the Japanese Government has always maintained an attitude of fairness and moderation, and did its best to reach a settlement, for which it made all possible concessions often in spite of great difficulties.

As for the China question which constituted an important subject of the negotiation, the Japanese Government showed a most conciliatory attitude.

As for the principle of Non-Discrimination in International Commerce, advocated by the American Government, the Japanese Government expressed its desire to see the said principle applied throughout the world, and declared that along with the actual practice of this principle in the world, the Japanese Government would endeavor to apply the same in the Pacific area, including China, and made it clear that Japan had no intention of excluding from China economic activities of third powers pursued on an equitable basis.

Furthermore, as regards the question of withdrawing troops from French Indo-China, the Japanese government even volunteered, as mentioned above, to carry out an immediate evacuation of troops from Southern French Indo-China as a measure of easing the situation.

JD:1–7143   Navy Trans. 12-6-41 (S)
25843

From: Tokyo
To: Washington
December 4, 1941
Purple
#902 (Part 7 of 14)

It is presumed that the spirit of conciliation exhibited to the utmost degree by the Japanese Government in all these matters is fully appreciated by the American Government.

On the other hand, the American government, always holding fast to theories in disregard of realities, and refusing to yield an inch on its impractical principles, caused undue delays in the negotiation. It is difficult to understand this attitude of the American government and the Japanese government desires to call the attention of the American government especially to the following points:

1. The American government advocates in the name of world peace those principles favorable to it and urges upon the Japanese government the acceptance thereof. The peace of the world may be brought about only by discovering a mutually acceptable formula through recognition of the reality of the situation and mutual appreciation of one another's position. An attitude such as ignores realities and imposes one's selfish views upon others will scarcely serve the purpose of facilitating the consummation of negotiations.
25843

[Secret]

From: Tokyo
To: Washington
December 6, 1941
Purple
#902 (Part 8 of 14)

Of the various principles put forward by the American government as a basis of the Japanese-American agreement, there are some which the Japanese government is ready to accept in principle, but in view of the world's actual conditions, it seems only a Utopian ideal, on the part of the American government, to attempt to force their immediate adoption.

Again, the proposal to conclude a multilateral non-agression pact between Japan, the United States, Great Britain, China, the Soviet Union, The Netherlands, and Thailand, which is patterned after the old concept of collective security, is far removed from the realities of East Asia.

The American proposal contains a stipulation which states: "Both governments will agree that no agreement, which either has concluded with any third powers, shall be interpreted by it in such a way as to conflict with the fundamental purpose of this agreement, the establishment and preservation of peace throughout the Pacific area." It is presumed that the above provision has been proposed with a view to restrain Japan from fulfilling its obligations under the Tripartite Pact when the United States participates in the war in Europe, and, as such, it cannot be accepted by the Japanese Government.

JD—1:7143   Navy Trans. 12-6-41 (S)
25843

From: Tokyo
To: Washington
December 6, 1941
Purple
#902 (Part 9 of 14)

The American Government, obsessed with its own views and opinions, may be said to be scheming for the extension of the war. While it seeks, on the one hand, to secure its rear by stabilizing the Pacific area, it is engaged, on the other hand, in aiding Great Britain and preparing to attack, in the name of self-defense, Germany and Italy two powers that are striving to establish a new order in Europe. Such a policy is totally at variance with the many principles upon which the American Government proposes to found the stability· of the Pacific area through peaceful means.

3. Where as the American Government under the principles it rigidly upholds, objects to settling international

issues through military pressure, it is exercising in conjunction with Great Britain and other nations pressure by economic power. Recourse to such pressure as a means of dealing with international relations should be condemned as it is at times more inhuman than military pressure.

JD–7143   Navy Trans. 12-6-41 (S)
25843

From: Tokyo
To: Washington
December 6, 1941
Purple
#902 (Part 10 of 14)

4. It is impossible not to reach the conclusion that the American Government desires to maintain and strengthen, in collusion with Great Britain and other powers, its dominant position it has hitherto occupied not only in China but in other areas of East Asia. It is a fact of history that one countr–(45 letters garbled or missing)–been compelled to observe the status quo under the Anglo-American policy of imperialistic exploitation and to sacrifice the –es to the prosperity of the two nations. The Japanese Government cannot tolerate the perpetuation of such a situation since it direcly runs counter to Japan's fundamental policy to enable all nations to enjoy each its proper place in the world.

JD1–7143   Navy Trans. 12-6-41 (S)
25843

From: Tokyo
To: Washington
December 6, 1941
Purple
#902 (Part 11 of 14)

The stipulation proposed by the American Government relative to French Indo-China is a good exemplification of the above-mentioned American policy. That the six countries,–Japan, the United States, Great Britain, The Netherlands, China and Thailand,–excepting France, should undertake among themselves to respect the territorial integrity and sovereignty of French Indo-China and equality of treatment in trade and commerce would be tantamount to placing that territory under the joint guarantee of the governments of those six countries. Apart from the fact that such a proposal totally ignores the position of France, it is unacceptable to the Japanese government in that such an arrangement cannot but be considered as an extension to French Indo-China of a system similar to the n—(50 letters missed)—sible for the present predicament of East Asia.

JD1–7153   Navy Trans. 12-6-41 (S)
25843

From: Tokyo
To: Washington
December 6, 1941
Purple
#902 (Part 12 of 14)

5. All the items demanded of Japan by the American government regarding China such as wholesale evacuation of troops or unconditional application of the principle of Non-Discrimination in International Commerce ignore the actual conditions of China, and are calculated to destroy Japan's position as the stabilizing factor of East Asia. The attitude of the American government in demanding Japan not to support militarily, politically or economically any regime other than the regime at Chungking, disregarding thereby the existence of the Nanking government, shatters the very basis of the present negotiation. This demand of the American government falling, as it does, in line with its above-mentioned refusal to cease from aiding the Chungking regime, demonstrates clearly the intention of the American government to obstruct the restoration of normal relations between Japan and China and the return of peace to East Asia.

JD—1: 7143   Navy Trans. 12-6-41 (S)
25843

From: Tokyo
To: Washington
December 6, 1941

Purple
#902 (Part 13 of 14)

5. In brief, the American proposal contains certain acceptable items such as those concerning commerce, including the conclusion of a trade agreement, mutual
removal of the freezing restrictions, and stabilization of
the Yen and Dollar exchange, or the abolition of extraterritorial rights in China. On the other hand, however,
the proposal in question ignores Japan's sacrifices in the
four years of the China Affair, menaces the empire's
existence itself and disparages its honour and prestige.
Therefore, viewed in its entirety, the Japanese government
regrets that it cannot accept the proposal as a basis of
negotiation.

6. The Japanese government, in its desire for an early
conclusion of the negotiation, proposed that simultaneously with the conclusion of the Japanese-American negotiation, agreements be signed with Great Britain and other
interested countries. The proposal was accepted by the
American government. However, since the American government has made the proposal of November 26th as a
result of frequent consultations with Great Britain, Australia, The Netherlands and Chungking, ANDND* presumably by catering to the wishes of the Chungking regime on
the questions of CHTUAL YLOKMMTT** be concluded
that all these countries are at one with the United States
in ignoring Japan's position.

JD–1: 7143   Navy Trans. 12-6-41 **(S)**
25843

From: Tokyo
To: Washington
7 December 1941
(Purple–Eng)
#902 Part 14 of 14

(NOTE.–In the forwarding instructions to the radio
station handling this part, appeared the plain English
phrase "VERY IMPORTANT")

*Probably "and as."
**Probably "China, can but."

7. Obviously it is the intention of the American Government to conspire with Great Britain and other countries to obstruct Japan's efforts toward the establishment of peace through the creation of a New Order in East Asia, and especially to preserve Anglo-American rights and interests by keeping Japan and China at war. This intention has been revealed clearly during the course of the present negotiations. Thus, the earnest hope of the Japanese Government to adjust Japanese-American relations and to preserve and promote the peace of the Pacific through cooperation with the American Government has finally been lost.

The Japanese Government regrets to have to notify hereby the American Government that in view of the attitude of the American Government it cannot but consider that it is impossible to reach an agreement through further negotiations.

25843

JD–1: 7143   (M) Navy trans. 7 Dec. 1941 (S–TT)

[Secret]

From: Tokyo
To: Washington
December 6, 1941
Purple
#904

Re my #902.

There is really no need to tell you this, but in the preparation of the aide memoire be absolutely sure not to use a typist or any other person.

Be most extremely cautious in preserving secrecy.

Army 25844

JD: 7144   Trans. 12-6-41 (S)

[Secret]

From: Tokyo
To: Washington
December 7, 1941
Purple (Urgent–Very Important)
#907 To be handled in government code

Re my #902.[a]

Will the Ambassador please submit to the United States Government (if possible to the Secretary of State) our reply to the United States at 1:00 p.m. on the 7th, your time.

Army 25850   Trans. 12/7/41 (S)

[a]S.I.S. #25843—text of Japanese reply.

Document No. 24

THE NAVY'S WAR WARNING [24]

Admiral Stark's war warning to Admiral Kimmel did not have the desired effect on the Hawaiian commander. He was merely confirmed in his belief, shared by other high Army and Navy officers as well as members of the administration, that war would break out in Southeast Asia.

γ γ γ

Top Secret

November 27, 1941.
From: Chief of Naval Operations
Action: CINCAF, CINCPAC
Info: CINCLANT, SPENAVO
272337

This despatch is to be considred a war warning X Negotiations with Japan looking toward stabilization of conditions in the Pacific have ceased and an aggressive move by Japan is expected within the next few days X The number and equipment of Japanese troops and the organization of naval task forces indicates an amphibious expedition against either the Philippines Thai or Kra peninsula or possibly Borneo X Execute an appropriate defensive deployment preparatory to carrying out the tasks assigned in WPL 46 X Inform district and army authorities X A similar warning is being sent by War Department X Spenavo inform British X Continental districts Guam Samoa directed take appropriate measures against sabotage.

Copy to WPD, War Dept.

[24] *Pearl Harbor Attack*, Part XIV, p. 1406.

THE ARMY'S WAR WARNING[25]

General Marshall's war warning to General Short was called by the latter a "Do-Don't" message. Short ordered a sabotage alert in response to it.

γ   γ   γ

Secret

Priority

Priority   *November 27, 1941.*

COMMANDING GENERAL,
    Hawaiian Department, Fort Shafter, T.H.

No. 472

Negotiations with Japan appear to be terminated to all practical purposes with only the barest possibilities that the Japanese Govenment might come back and offer to continue Period Japanese future action unpredictable but hostile action possible at any moment Period If hostilities cannot comma repeat cannot comma be avoided the United States desires that Japan commit the first overt act Period This policy should not comma repeat not comma be construed as restricting you to a course of action that might jeopardize your defense Period Prior to hostile Japanese action you are directed to undertake such reconnaissance and other measures as you deem necessary but these measures should be carried out so as not comma repeat not comma to alarm civil population or disclose intent Period Report measures taken Period Should hostilities occur you will carry out the tasks assigned in rainbow five so far as they pertain to Japan Period Limit dissemination of this highly secret information to minimum essential officers

MARSHALL

War Department message center: Please send same radiogram to: Commanding General, Caribbean Defense Command, Quarry Heights, C.Z.

[25]*Pearl Harbor Attack*, Part XIV, p. 1328.

GENERAL MARSHALL'S FINAL WARNING [26]

The following message, which left Washington at 12:18 p.m., was transmitted by commercial means and did not reach Pearl Harbor until after the raid had begun.

γ   γ   γ

Secret

1549WS Washington DC 74/73 RCA USG ETAT 7 1218P.

C G

Hawn Dept Ft. Shafter, T.H.

529 7th   Japanese are presenting at one pm eastern standard time today what amounts to an ultimatum also they are under orders to destroy their code machine immediately stop just what significance the hour set may have we do not know but be on alert accordingly stop inform naval authorities of this communication

MARSHALL.

[26] *Pearl Harbor Attack*, Part XIV, p. 1334.

Document No. 27

THE MORI CALL[27]

The intercepted telephone conversation between a Japanese dentist, Dr. Motokazu Mori, in Honolulu, and a contact in Tokyo was shown to General Short on December 6 but failed to alarm him.

γ   γ   γ

(Handwritten note:) Telephone conversation of Dec. 3, 1941 between a citizen in Honolulu (Japanese) & a military or naval officer in Tokyo. Translated & available to Military intel. Hawaii, Dec. 5, 1944.

IC (J) Hello, is this Mori?

(H) Hello, this is Mori.

(J) I am sorry to have troubled you. Thank you very much.

(H) Not at all.

(J) I received your telegram and was able to grasp the essential points. I would like to have your impressions on the conditions you are observing at present. Are airplanes flying daily?

(H) Yes, lots of them fly around.

(J) Are they large planes?

(H) Yes, they are quite big.

(J) Are they flying from morning till night?

(H) Well, not to that extent, but last week they were quite active in the air.

(J) I hear there are many sailors there, is that right?

(H) There aren't so many now. There were more in the beginning part of this year and the ending part of last year.

(J) Is that so?

[2]   (H) I do not know why this is so, but it appears that there are very few sailors here at present.

(J) Are any Japanese people there holding meeting to discuss US-Japanese negotiations being conducted presently?

[27]*Pearl Harbor Attack,* Part XV, pp. 167-69.

176

(H) No, not particularly. The minds of the Japa- here appear calmer than expected. They are getting along harmoniously.

(J) Don't the American community look with suspicion on the Japanese?

(H) Well, we hardly notice any of them looking on us with suspicion. This fact is rather unexpected. We are not hated or despised. The soldiers here and we get along very well. All races are living in harmony. It appears that the people who come here change to feel like the rest of the people here. There are some who say odd things, but these are limited to newcomers from the mainland, and after staying here from three to six months, they too begin to think and feel like the rest of the pople in the islands.

(J) That's fine.

(H) Yes, it's fine, but we feel a bit amused.

(J) Has there been any increase in . . .? . . . of late? That is, as a result of the current tense situation.

[3]   (H) There is nothing which stands out, but the city is enjoying a war building boom.

(J) What do you mean by enjoying a war building boom?

(H) Well, a boom in many fields. Although there is no munitions industry here engaged in by the army, civilian workers are building houses for the army personnel. Most of the work here is directed towards building houses of various sorts. There are not enough carpenters, electricians and plumbers. Students at the High School and University have quit school and are working on these jobs, regardless of the fact that they are unskilled in this work.

(J) Are there many big factories there?

(H) No, there are no factories, but a lot of small buildings of various kinds are being constructed.

(J) Is that so?

(H) It is said that the population of Honolulu has doubled that of last year.

(J) What is the population?

(H) About 200,000 to 240,000. Formerly there were about 150,000 people.

(J) What about night time?

(H) There seem to be precautionary measures taken.

(J) What about searchlights?

(H) Well, not much to talk about.

[4[(J) Do they put searchlights on when planes fly about at night?

(H) No.

(J) What about the Honolulu newspapers?

(H) The comments by the papers are pretty bad. They are opposite to the atmosphere pervading the city. I don't know whether the newspaper is supposed to lead the community or not, but they carry headlines pertaining to Japan daily. The main articles concern the US-Japanese conferences.

(J) What kind of impression did Mr. Kurusu make in Hawaii?

(H) A very good one. Mr. Kurusu understands the American mind, and he was very adept at answering queries of the press.

(J) Are there any Japanese people there who are planning to evacuate Hawaii?

(H) There are almost none wishing to do that.

(J) What is the climate there now?

(H) These last few days have been very cold with occasional rainfall, a phenomena very rare in Hawaii. Today, the wind is blowing very strongly, a very unusual climate.

(J) Is that so?

(H) Here is something interesting. Litvinoff, the Russian ambassador to the United States, arrived here yesterday. I believe he enplaned for the mainland today. He made no statements on any problems.

(J) Did he make any statements concerning the US-Japan question?

[5] (H) No. Not only did he not say anything regarding the US-Japan question, he also did not mention anything pertaining to the Russo-German war. It appears he was ordered by his government not to make any statement.

(J) Well, that means he was very different from Mr. Kurusu.

(H) Yes.

(J) What kind of impression did Litvinoff make?

(H) A very good one here. He impressed the people as being very quiet and a gentleman.

(J) Did he stop at the same hotel as Mr. Kurusu?

(H) Yes, at the Royal Hawaiian overnight. He has already enplaned for the mainland.

(J) Do you know anything about the United States fleet?

(H) No, I don't know anything about the fleet. Since we try to avoid talking about such matters, we do not know much about the fleet. At any rate, the fleet here seems small. I don't all of the fleet has done this, but it seems that the fleet has left here.

(J) Is that so? What kind of flowers are in bloom in Hawaii at present?

(H) Presently, the flowers in bloom are fewest out of the whole year. However, the hibiscus and the poinsettia are in bloom now.

*(J) Does not seem to know about poinsettias. He admits he doesn't know.

(J) Do you feel any inconvenience there due to the suspension of importation of Japanese goods?

[6]   (H) Yes, we feel the invonvenience very much. There are no Japanese soy, and many other foodstuffs which come from Japan. Although there are enough foodstuffs (Japanese) left in stock to last until February of next year, at any rate it is a big inconvenience.

(J) What do you lack most?

(H) I believe the soy is what everyone is worried about most. Since the freeze order is in force, the merchants who have been dealing in Japanese goods are having a hard time.

(J) Thanks very much.

(H) By the way, here is something interesting about Hawaii. Liquor sells very fast due to the boom here. The United States, which twenty years ago went under prohibition, is today flooded by liquor. British and French liquors are being sold. The Japanese merchants, whose business came to a standstill due to the suspension of importation of Japanese goods, engage in liquor manufacture. The rice from the United States is used in brewing Japanese sake here, and the sake is exported back to the mainland.

*(H) explains that the Japanese sake brewed in Honolulu is called "Takara-Masamune", that a person named Takagishi was the technical expert in charge of the brewing; that said Takagishi is a son-on-law of Grand Chamberlain Hyakutake, being married to the latter's daughter; and that said Takagishi returned recently to Japan on the Taiyo Maru. He adds that Japanese here and the Americans also drink sake. He informs (J) that Japanese chrysanthemums are in full bloom here, and that there are no herring-roe for this year's New Year celebration.

(J)   How many first generation Japanese are there in Hawaii according to last surveys made?

[7]   (H) About fifty thousand.

(J) How about the second generation Japanese?

(H) About 120,000 or 130,000.

(J)   How many out of this number of second generation Japanese are in the United States Army?

(H) There aren't so many up to the present. About 1,500 have entered the army, and the majority of those who have been drafted into the army are Japanese.

(J) Any first generation Japanese in the army?

(H) No. They do not draft any first generation Japanese.

(J) Is that right, that there are 1,500 in the army?

(H) Yes, that is true up to the present, but may increase since more will be inducted in January.

(J) Thank you very much.

(H) Not at all. I'm sorry I couldn't be of much use.

(J) Oh no, that was fine. Best regards to your wife.

(H) Wait a moment, please?

(J) Off phone.

Document No. 28

TESTIMONY ABOUT THE SIGHTING AND SINKING OF JAPANESE MIDGET SUBMARINES ON DECEMBER 7, 1941[28]

The following excerpts from the testimony of Captains William W. Outerbridge and John Bayliss Earle before the Hewitt Inquiry, and of Lieutenant Commander Harold Kaminski before the Roberts Commission illustrate the failure of the alert system at Hawaii. Outerbridge testified on May 21, 1945; Earle, on June 19, 1945; and Kaminski, on January 8, 1942.

γ   γ   γ

Captain Outerbridge's Testimony

Admiral HEWITT. You were the Commanding Officer of the WARD on the morning of 7 December 1941?

Captain OUTERBRIDGE. Yes, sir.

Admiral HEWITT. And during the early hours of that morning, you had several actual contacts with submarines? Is that so?

Captain OUTERBRIDGE. Several actual contacts?

Admiral HEWITT. Well, reported contacts.

Captain OUTERBRIDGE. Yes sir. We had one alert and one actual contact and then later, after the attack, we had several outside.

Admiral HEWITT. And during the early hours of that the conversation which you had with the CONDOR along about 0520 Honolulu time and later there is in evidence the report of your actual attack on the submarine. Will you give me your story of the events of the morning, beginning with the report from the CONDOR about 0400?

Captain OUTERBRIDGE. That doesn't appear on this record, but she signalled us by flashing light that she believed she had seen an object that looked like a submarine proceeding to the westward, and I believe she had just

---

[28]*Pearl Harbor Attack,* Part XXXVI, pp. 55-58, 267-70; Part XXIII, pp. 1034-38.

come out and was sweeping, magnetic sweep out in the channel, but she said, "The submarine is standing to the westward."

Admiral HEWITT. What was her location?

Captain OUTERBRIDGE. She was in the channel, sweeping with her magnetic sweeps.

Admiral HEWITT. The approach channel to Pearl Harbor?

Captain OUTERBRIDGE. Outside the actual channel, between the reefs, but on the approach channel to Pearl Harbor.

Admiral HEWITT. Swept channel?

Captain OUTERBRIDGE. Swept channel, yes, and we went to General Quarters and proceeded to her position, as close as we could get to her without fouling her sweeping gear, and then we stood to the westward, slowed to ten knots, and searched. It was a sonar search. We couldn't see anything.

Admiral HEWITT. About what time did you get that signal?

Captain OUTERBRIDGE. We got that signal about 0358, visual signal about 0358, and we searched for about an hour and didn't find anything; so I got in contact with her again and asked her for a verification. Then she said— this is in the record here. We asked her first, "What was the approximate distance and course of the submarine that you sighted?" and she said, "the course was about what we were steering at the time 020 magnetic and about 1000 yards from the entrance apparently heading for the entrance." Well, I knew then that we had been searching in the wrong direction. We went to westward, and, of course, there was still doubt as to whether she had actually seen a submarine because there hadn't been any other conversation, except by flashing light with us, and I wondered whether they were sure or not; so I did ask them, "Do you have any additional information on the sub?" and they said, "No additional information," and I then asked them, "When was the last time approximately that you saw the submarine?" and they said, "Approximate time 0350 and he was apparently heading for the entrance." Then we thanked them for their information and asked them to notify us if they had any more information and then we just kept on searching in our area, in the restricted area outside of the buoys. That was the end of this incident for the first search.

Admiral HEWITT. You made no report of that to higher authority?

Captain OUTERBRIDGE. No, sir, I didn't make any report of it.

Admiral HEWITT. What was your evaluation of that?

Captain OUTERBRIDGE. Well, at the time I thought perhaps it wasn't a submarine, because they didn't report it. This conversation was taken over another circuit entirely. This is not in either his log or mine. They didn't report it and I thought if he didn't report it, he must not think it is a submarine. It was his initial report and I thought it may not be. It may have been anything; it may have been a buoy. Since then, I don't believe it was a buoy. I believe the Commanding Officer of the CONDOR saw a submarine. I don't know where he is. I think he was killed, killed in action. But at that time I didn't know whether or not it was a submarine.

Admiral HEWITT. You say you think the Commanding Officer of the CONDOR was killed?

Captain OUTERBRIDGE. I believe he was killed.

Admiral HEWITT. Do you remember his name?

Captain OUTERBRIDGE. No Sir, I don't know, but I met some people who told me about him.

Admiral HEWITT. Well, now about the later contact.

Captain OUTERBRIDGE. The later contact—I turned in again and was sleeping in the emergency cabin, as usual, and Lieutenant Goepner had the deck. He was a j. g. He called me and said, "Captain, come on the bridge." The helmsman was the first one to sight this object and he saw this thing moving. It looked like a buoy to him, but they watched it and after they had watched it for a while, they decided probably it was a conning tower of a submarine, although we didn't have anything that looked like it in our Navy, and they had never seen anything like it. I came on the bridge as fast as I could and took a look at it. I don't know where it appeared to them at first, but at that time it appeared to me to be following the ANTARES in. The ANTARES had been reported to me and at that time I thought the ANTARES had been heading into the harbor. She also had a tow, towing a lighter, and it appeared to me the submarine was following astern of the tow.

Admiral HEWITT. Astern of the tow?

Captain OUTERBRIDGE. Yes, sir. It may or may not have been. I think other people can testify it was standing in to Honolulu. To me it appeared to be following the ANTARES in and I thought, "She is going to follow the ANTARES in, whatever it is." It was going fairly fast. I thought she was making about twelve knots. It seemed to be a little fast to me. I was convinced it was a submarine. I was convinced it couldn't be anything else. It must be a submarine and it wasn't anything that we had and we also had a message that any submarine operating in the restricted area—not operating in the submarine areas and not escorted—should be attacked. We had that message; so there was no doubt at all in my mind what to do. So, we went to General Quarters again and attacked. That was 0740-0640.

Admiral HEWITT. And you attacked and you reported, I believe that—

Captain OUTERBRIDGE. Yes, sir, we reported.

Admiral HEWITT. Will you identify those exchanges of messages? Will you identify the messages on the radio log?

Captain OUTERBRIDGE. Yes, sir. The Executive Officer was on the bridge at the time. We made the attack and we dropped depth charges in front of the submarine. The first report was, "We have dropped depth charges upon sub operating in defensive sea area." I thought, "Well, now, maybe I had better be more definite," because we did fire and if we said we fired, people would know it was on the surface, because saying it was a sub and dropping depth charges, they may have said it might have been a blackfish or a whale. So I said, "We have attacked fired upon and dropped depth charges upon submarine operating in defensive sea area," so they would feel, well, he shot at something. We sent the message at 0653, the second one. . . .

Admiral HEWITT. What do you feel was the effect of your attack?

Captain OUTERBRIDGE. I think we sank the submarine.

Admiral HEWITT. What do you base that on?

Captain OUTERBRIDGE. On the gun hit, only on the gun hit.

Admiral HEWITT. There was a gun hit on it?

Captain OUTERBRIDGE. There was a gun hit on it, and I looked these submarines over and there is no hatch between the conning tower and the tube of the submarine, where I believe it was a hit, right at the waterline, the base of the conning tower.

Admiral HEWITT. And the submarine disappeared after that?

Captain OUTERBRIDGE. Yes, sir, it disappeared.

Admiral HEWITT. That was before you made the depth charge attack?

Captain OUTERBRIDGE. Yes, sir, we fired at the submarine before we made the depth charge attack, and as she was going under the stern, we dropped over the depth charges.

Admiral HEWITT. Your depth charges were close to her?

Captain OUTERBRIDGE. Yes, sir.

Admiral HEWITT. Definitely?

Captain OUTERBRIDGE. Definitely, they were there. I didn't claim a kill—

Admiral HEWITT. Whom were those reports addressed to?

Captain OUTERBRIDGE. I believe it was Commander Inshore Patrol. We were working for inshore patrol, but the interpretation is here—

Admiral HEWITT. You got the calls?

Captain OUTERBRIDGE. Yes, sir, we got the calls.

Admiral HEWITT. Do you remember what they mean?

Captain OUTERBRIDGE. No, sir.

Admiral HEWITT. Those were the only reports of that attack you made?

Captain OUTERBRIDGE. Yes, sir, two messages on that.

Admiral HEWITT. What was your action after the completion of that attack?

Captain OUTERBRIDGE. Well, I saw one of these large white sampans lying to out there in the defensive area?

Admiral HEWITT. Was that against regulations?

Captain OUTERBRIDGE. That was against standing rules. They weren't supposed to be in the defensive area, but he was in there. So, I turned around and went after him and we chased him towards Barber's Point. He was going pretty fast.

Admiral HEWITT. He tried to get away from you?

Captain OUTERBRIDGE. It appeared that way to me. He could have stopped much sooner, but he appeared to be going around Barber's Point. When we did catch up to him, he came up waving a white flag. I thought that was funny. I thought, "We will just send for the Coast Guard." That was what we always did when we caught a sampan in the defensive area. We sent for the Coast Guard and they were very prompt. They sent a cutter out to take him in.

Admiral HEWITT. Will you identify for the record those two messages you sent about the sampan, which are on the Bishop's Point record?

Captain OUTERBRIDGE. "We have intercepted a sampan into Honolulu. Please have Coast Guard send cutter to relieve us of sampan." And, "We have intercepted sampan and escorting sampan into Honolulu. Please have cutter relieve us of sampan." We sent that. That is a little garbled, but that looks like it.

Admiral HEWITT. What was the time of it?

Captain OUTERBRIDGE. That was 0833 and 0835.

Lieutenant Commander Kaminski's Testimony

Admiral STANDLEY. What duty were you performing on the night of December 6 and the morning of December 7?

Commander KAMINSKI. I was District Watch Officer.

Admiral STANDLEY. From what time?

Commander KAMINSKI. I had the watch at 4 o'clock Saturday.

Admiral STANDLEY. Four p.m. Saturday?

Commander KAMINSKI. Yes.

Admiral STANDLEY. 1600?

Commander KAMINSKI. Yes, 1600 Saturday night. I stayed on continuously for three days after that.

Admiral STANDLEY. What was your tour of duty?

Commander KAMINSKI. My duty at that time was that I was the officer in charge of net and boom defenses.

Admiral STANDLEY. I mean so far as your watch duty on that night was concerned. You went on watch at 1600?

Commander KAMINSKI. Yes.

Admiral STANDLEY. When would you be relieved, ordinarily?

Commander KAMINSKI. I would ordinarily be relieved at 1 o'clock the next morning, sir, Sunday morning.

Admiral STANDLEY. Were you the only officer on watch at that time?

Commander KAMINSKI. Yes, I was the only officer on duty in the district. However, they had the yard watch and then the security watch, but at that time I was the only officer on watch.

Admiral STANDLEY. What were your duties as watch officer?

Commander KAMINSKI. Well, my duties as watch officer were to take care of anything that turned up pertaining to the district—any district activities.

Admiral STANDLEY. Had there been any calls made upon you as duty officer which could not be performed at any time prior to that time?

188 PEARL HARBOR: THE CONTINUING CONTROVERSY

Commander KAMINSKI. I do not understand.

Admiral STANDLEY. Had you been standing watch prior to December 6?

Commander KAMINSKI. Yes.

Admiral STANDLEY. Had any occasions ever arisen when any matters came up which could not be handled?

Commander KAMINSKI. No, sir.

Admiral STANDLEY. When you went on watch you relieved the officer who was on duty?

Commander KAMINSKI. Yes.

Admiral STANDLEY. You understood what your duties were supposed to be?

Commander KAMINSKI. Yes.

Admiral STANDLEY. Did you have any idea that you could not perform them under any circumstances?

Commander KAMINSKI. I felt that the station could not function efficiently with just myself. I felt that before. I had complained about the man they had on the telephone watch, and they had Hawaiians there who were not able to speak plain English and they did not receive the proper instructions at the telephone. In fact, the man I had that morning was perfectly useless and had not been instructed, and they did not understand the teletype there, and I felt that the situation should be corrected and we should have more personnel and the teletype should be manned and not just one officer with one enlisted man.

Admiral STANDLEY. Did your instructions call for any increase of help in case of emergency?

Commander KAMINSKI. No, my instructions in case of emergency were to call the Commandant; to call his aide, as a matter of fact, and second, if I could—no, that is wrong.

My first instructions were to call the chief of staff and the Commandant's aide. Those were the first to call: the chief of staff and the Commandant's aide.

Admiral STANDLEY. Did you have other calls that you were required to make?

Commander KAMINSKI. Constantly we had various routine calls. For instance there might be a destroyer coming in or something with contagious diseases and there might be various inspections and dispatches coming in. It was a regular routine duty.

Admiral STANDLEY. You received a call that morning of the sinking of a submarine?

Commander KAMINSKI. Yes. I have the original dispatch and I initialed it.

Admiral STANDLEY. What was the time?

Commander KAMINSKI. The time I received it? I initialed it. I saved a copy of it and I have it in this file.

Admiral STANDLEY. What was the time?

Commander KAMINSKI. 0712. (Reading :)

From: WARD.
To: COM 14.
  We have attacked fired upon and dropped charges upon submarine operating in defensive sea area.

Admiral STANDLEY. What did you do when you received that message?

Commander KAMINSKI. When I received that message I endeavored to get in touch with the Commandant's aide. I could not reach him on the telephone. I then got in touch with the Cincus's duty officer. I read the message to him. I then got in touch with the chief of staff.

I have it here in chronological order.

Admiral STANDLEY. Just tell us what you did. How long did it take you to get in touch with the chief of staff?

Commander KAMINSKI. It took me quite a while to get him. I have some other message in here.

These are the reconstructed notes the next morning. During the morning of December 7 at 0712 I received that dispatch from the WARD, which I just read. Upon receiving that dispatch, I immediately endeavored to raise the Commandant's aide and could not contact him. I called and contacted Cincpac Duty Officer and read him the dispatch.

Admiral STANDLEY. Do you have the time when that call was made?

Commander KAMINSKI. No, because it was practically the same time. I did not waste much time. It was right after I got it. I did that next.

General McCOY. It was all within a few minutes?

Commander KAMINSKI. Yes.

I called and contacted the Cincpac Duty Officer and read him the dispatch. I sent the message to ready duty destroyer MAHAN.

I have in here the MAHAN, but it was the MONO—GHAN and they got it.

It was, "Get under way immediately and contact U.S.S. WARD in defensive sea area."

Admiral STANDLEY. Just a minute. Did you send that message on your own responsibility?

Commander KAMINSKI. Yes.

Admiral STANDLEY. Do you have instructions that that is what you are to do?

Commander KAMINSKI. I had instructions, yes, to use my own judgment. I knew it was a ready duty destroyer, so I sent that message out. It was by visual.

I had the MAHAN, but the MONAGHAN went out. They knew it was meant for the ready duty destroyer. I told them to get under way and contact the U.S.S. WARD in defensive sea area. That is the message I sent.

I instructed the communication office to send a copy of the last message to the U.S.S. WARD for information. I wanted to let the WARD know that I had that information.

I then called the chief of staff, Captain Earle, notifying him of the WARD'S message. All this occurred prior to calling the chief of staff.

He requested confirmation from the WARD, which I relayed to the WARD and never received an answer; but I received a second dispatch in the interim about the time which I will give to you. It was between 0712 and 0720 that I received this dispatch. That dispatch is:

> We have intercepted a sampan. We are escorting this sampan into Honolulu. Please inform Coast Guard to send cutter for relieve us of sampan.

That should be "to relieve us of sampan" instead of "for relieve us of sampan." That is garbled.

Admiral STANDLEY. That came in from the WARD?

Commander KAMINSKI. Yes, the U.S.S. WARD.

Admiral STANDLEY. Then what happened?

Commander KAMINSKI. I got in touch with the Coast Guard and found that they had received a communication practically simultaneous with mine; they had picked it up, so I dropped it.

Then I called the War Plans Officer, Commander Momsen, because after I called Captain Earle, he was quite astounded and he said he could not believe it. He asked for this confirmation. He asked to send him that confirmation, and he made several remarks at that time that he was astounded and that it was unbelievable, and made various other remarks.

He asked me to notify the Commandant. I asked him if he would please notify the Commandant because I had other messages to put through. He said he would. I had other messages to put through and asked him if he would do it. He notified the Commandant.

He suggested about calling Commander Momsen. I called the War Plans Officer, Commander Momsen, and was ordered to call Ensign Logan. He arrived at approximately 0725. Of course, these times are approximate and were reconstructed, and they are accurate to the best of my ability.

I called Commander Momsen around 0720, sir. I called Ensign Logan immediately after, in about five minutes.

It was 0725 that I received the message from the WARD. That is the sampan message. All these things were almost simultaneous.

A minute after, I got the Coast Guard; could not contact an officer but was informed by communications officer of the 14th Naval District that Coast Guard had received WARD's second message simultaneously. Commander Momsen arrived in the operations office a few minutes after Ensign Logan.

I then called my own commanding officer. After that, with the assistance of the lady at the switchboard I started to call all the department heads, after arranging with the telephone office to keep the lines open.

Captain Earle's Testimony

Mr. SONNETT. Referring to the morning of December 7, 1941, Captain, I show you exhibit 18 of this investigation and direct your attention particularly to the conversation recorded at about 0520 Pearl Harbor time of that date between the WARD and the CONDOR, and ask whether that conversation or the fact of such a conversation came to your attention prior to the attack on December 7th?

Captain EARLE. It did not.

Mr. SONNETT. You will note on the second page of that exhibit, Captain, a report by the WARD of its attack upon a submarine. That report did come to your attention prior to the attack, as I understand your previous testimony.

Captain EARLE. That report did come to my attention but not in the wording that it is included in the log of the section base.

Mr. SONNETT. Would you state, Captain, the report of that conversation which was received by you in December 7, 1941, and state the time approximately at which you received it?

Captain EARLE. About 0710 I was informed by the Operations Duty Officer, Lieutenant Commander Kaminski, that he had received a message from the WARD to the effect that "We have attacked and fired on a submarine."

Admiral HEWITT. Nothing about depth charges?

Captain EARLE. No, sir.

Mr. SONNETT. That report, Captain, was a more specific report, was it not, than any previous report concerning a submarine contact which had been received by you?

Captain EARLE. Yes.

Mr. SONNETT. What action was taken on the report?

Captain EARLE. As I recall it, I immediately told the watch officer to inform the Commander-in-Chief's Operation Officer and to take steps to get the relief destroyer ready to proceed out of the harbor, to get the message checked and verified and attempt to find out what further action was being taken by the WARD. I then called the Commandant of the Fourteenth Naval District, Admiral Bloch, informed him of what had been done, and talked the situation over with him for some time with a view to deciding what other action should be taken. Our reaction was that it was probably a mistake as we had had numerous reports of sighting of submarines, but that if it were not a mistake, the WARD could take care of the situation and the relief destroyer could lend a hand, while the Commander-in-Chief had the necessary power to undertake any other action which might be desired. Mainly we were trying to definitely determine what had happened.

Mr. SONNETT. I take it, Captain, that no further action was taken on that report prior to the air attack on December 7th?

Captain EARLE. No other action was taken by me. I believe that in addition to that, that Commander Momsen, who was the Operations Officer, was contacted and told to take station. We were vaguely alarmed but could see no specific threat involved except that by the possible position of an enemy submarine in that area.

Mr. SONNETT. Captain, I show you exhibit 8 of the Naval Court of Inquiry, which is Pacific Fleet Confidential Letter number 2CL–41 (Revised), dated October 14, 1941, and ask whether you saw that and were familiar with that prior to December 7, 1941?

Captain EARLE. It is my recollection that I saw this before December 7, 1941....

Mr. SONNETT. Now, Captain, coming back to the previous question, it appears, does it not, that one of the assumptions of the security letter was that a declaration of war might be preceded by a surpise Japanese attack? Having that in mind and turning to the statement that you previously read concerning the presence of a submarine, will you state why, on the morning of December 7, 1941, upon receipt of the report from the WARD, it was not believed that a large Japanese force might be in the offing and why appropriate action was not taken on that belief?

Captain EARLE. In the first place, we were not sure of this supposed contact. It still seemed to have a possibility of being in error. This was particularly strengthened by a later report received from the WARD which said that she was proceeding to escort a sampan toward Honolulu. We couldn't imagine that the WARD, having actually attacked a submarine, would leave her post to proceed to Honolulu if it were a real attack. In the second place, we had no force immediately available to resist any attack as far as the District was concerned, except the relief destroyer, and we felt that by referring the matter to the Commander-in-Chief, that we had done all that we possibly could even if the attack were real.

TESTIMONY ABOUT THE RADAR CONTACT WITH THE JAPANESE PLANES [29]

The testimony of First Lieutenant Joseph L. Lockard and of Lieutenant Colonel Kermit A. Tyler before the Army Pearl Harbor Board on August 17, 1944 illustrates the failure of the Army to make proper use of the first radar contact with the Japanese planes about to attack Pearl Harbor. On December 7, 1941, Lockard was a Third Class Specialist and Tyler a 1st Lieutenant.

γ   γ   γ

Lieutenant Lockard's Testimony

63. General FRANK. You were at the set on the morning of December 7, were you?

Lieutenant LOCKARD. Yes, sir.

64. General FRANK. When did you go there?

Lieutenant LOCKARD. We went up the night before.

65. General FRANK. Did the set start operating on the morning of December 7th?

Lieutenant LOCKARD. Yes, sir. We started operation.

66. General FRANK. What time?

Lieutenant LOCKARD. Around four o'clock.

[*1023*] General FRANK. Who operated the set? Who was at the oscilloscope?

Lieutenant LOCKARD. I was.

68. General FRANK. From what time until what time?

Lieutenant LOCKARD. The whole period.

69. General FRANK. When did you start?

Lieutenant LOCKARD. At what time?

70. General FRANK. Yes.

Lieutenant LOCKARD. Around four o'clock.

71. General FRANK. What was picked up that morning and at what times, so far as your memory will serve you?

[29] *Pearl Harbor Attack,* Part XVII, pp. 531-33, 568-70.

Lieutenant LOCKARD. It was a rather dull morning. There was not much activity.

72. General FRANK. Up until what time? Did you pick up any planes before seven o'clock?

Lieutenant LOCKARD. If we did, sir, it was one or two or a small number.

73. General FRANK. When did you pick up this flight that was coming in from the north?

Lieutenant LOCKARD. Around 7:02.

74. General FRANK. What were the circumstances surrounding the situation as it existed? Were you at the oscilloscope, or was Elliott?

Lieutenant LOCKARD. I was still at the oscilloscope, sir. We were going to close down, but we figured that we might as well play around, because the truck had not come in yet to take us back for chow. So I was just checking the adjustments and was going to let Elliott operate them a while. He had not been in the outfit very long; he was a new man with us. I was going to let him operate. To me it looked like two main pulses. That is why I thought there was something wrong with the equipment, and I was checking to see if there was anything wrong. Apparently there was not.

75. General FRANK. Proceed and tell us what happened.

Lieutenant LOCKARD. Well, I showed it to Elliott. I fooled around some more trying to determine exactly whether it was something coming in or whether it was a defect in the equipment, and finally decided that it must be a flight of some sort. Since it was the only activity we had had that morning, I decided to plot it. Elliott plotted it.

76. General FRANK. Who did the plotting?

Lieutenant LOCKARD. Elliott. We picked it up at 136 miles, and when it got to 132 we called the information center—it was just a few minutes after seven—and there was no one. I knew the switchboard operator there, and I asked if there was anyone around.

77. General FRANK. You called the information center, or did the other man?

Lieutenant LOCKARD. No, sir. I was watching the track, and he made the phone call, and the switchboard operator told us there was no one around; so we asked him to look around; and, contrary to regulations, he left the switchboard and looked, and he found someone; but first, we told him about what we had, and he told this individual.

78. General FRANK. Do you know who that was?

Lieutenant LOCKARD. No, sir; I had never seen him.

79. General FRANK. You do not know whom he told?

Lieutenant LOCKARD. I know his name. I think I know his name.

80. General FRANK. What was it?

Lieutenant LOCKARD. Miller. I believe he was a liaison officer.

81. General FRANK. Miller, or Twler?

Lieutenant LOCKARD. The best that I can remember, sir, it was Miller.

82. General FRANK. All right.

Lieutenant LOCKARD. This individual—well, the switchboard operator came back and said that, "O.K.—it's all right," something to that effect. I can't tell you the conversation any more, because I haven't too good a memory; and we insisted—I asked—

83. General FRANK. You insisted what?

Lieutenant LOCKARD. I asked the switchboard operator if I couldn't speak to this person; which I did; and I gave him all the information that we had—the direction, the mileage, and the apparent size of whatever it was; and that was about the end of it, right there.

84. General FRANK. What did he tell you?

Lieutenant LOCKARD. Well—

85. General GRUNERT. Your are not incriminating anybody. Tell us. What did he tell you? Did he say, "Forget it," or that it did not amount to anything, or what?

Lieutenant LOCKARD. Something to that effect. I mean, "O.K."

86. General FRANK. Did he tell you to forget it, or what did he say?

Lieutenant LOCKARD. Well, he didn't—he wasn't very committal. He just said, "O.K.," or something to that effect—"You needn't"—

87. General FRANK. When you picked it up and had followed it, so that it had come from 137 or thereabouts down to a shorter distance from the sight, what did the oscilloscope show? Did it show that it was a single plane, or that it was a large group of planes? What was your interpretation if it?

Lieutenant LOCKARD. Well, sir, it was the largest group I had ever seen on the oscilloscope. It looked, as I said, like a main pulse, and that is why I was confused, at first, as to whether it was a flight or not. I had never seen one. It maybe was the exceptional reception in that particular spot, but it still produced the largest echo on the 'scope that I had seen.

88. General FRANK. Did you tell the man, then, at the information center, that it looked like an unusually large number of planes?

Lieutenant LOCKARD. Yes, sir.

89. General FRANK. And that didn't seem to excite him in any way?

Lieutenant LOCKARD. No, sir.

90. General FRANK. What followed from then on? Did you continue?

Lieutenant LOCKARD. Well, sir, we went as far as we thought was reasonably safe in our argument.

91. General FRANK. What do you mean? In your argument with whom? With the man at the information center?

Lieutenant LOCKARD. Yes, sir.

92. General FRANK. All right.

Lieutenant LOCKARD. Then we continued to follow the flight, and to plot it, till it got within about 22 miles—20 to 22 miles of the Island, at which time we lost it in this blacked-out area. Then we proceeded to close down the station and go back to Kawailoa for breakfast. The truck had arrived—or, had not arrived, yet, but there was nothing else working.

Colonel Tyler's Testimony

General FRANK. So on this morning, you were assigned there for instructional purposes, to learn about being a pursuit officer?

Colonel TYLER. Yes, sir.

16. General FRANK. Who was there, this morning, to teach you anything about that?

Colonel TYLER. I was the senior—in fact, I was the only officer there, and all that I could learn would be what I would learn by observing. By that I mean, there were about five or six plotters placing the plots (arrows) on the board, and there was a—

17. General FRANK. Was it a very well organized activity for the purpose of giving you instruction?

Colonel TYLER. I would say that the previous tour that I had through the information center was clear enough in giving me a set-up of the thing, but actually, there being no officers there to identify plots, nor no senior controller there, then, I wouldn't say that I was very well instructed that morning.

18. General FRANK. All right. Was the aircraft warning service, including the information center, operating that morning?

Colonel TYLER. Yes, sir; it was.

19. General FRANK. Were there any plots made on the board prior to 7 o'clock?

Colonel TYLER. I am quite sure there were, sir. There were a number of plots around the Island. As to whether they were just before 7, or started appearing about 7, I am not certain as to that.

20. General FRANK. Do you remember the occasion on which a flight from the north was picked up by the Opana station?

Colonel TYLER. Yes, sir.

21. General FRANK. You remember that?

Colonel TYLER. Yes, sir.

22. General FRANK. Will you give us the circumstances surrounding that? Can you give us a narrative concerning it?

Colonel TYLER. Just as a matter of interest, I saw this lad who was keeping the historical record. There is a record made of every plot that comes into the station, and I had not yet observed that activity, so I went over to see what he was doing, and it happened to be just about 7 o'clock, or roughly thereabout; and there were other plots on the board at that time. It was just about 7, or a little bit after, I think, and then, right at 7 o'clock, all the people who were in the information center, except the telephone operator, folded up their equipment and left. There were just the operator and myself again; and about 7:15, the radar operator from Opana called the telephone operator to say that he had a larger plot than he had ever seen before, on his 'scope, and the telephone operator relayed the call to me; so I took the call, and, inasmuch as I had no means of identifying friendly plots from enemy, nor was I led to believe that there would be any occasion to do so, I told him not to worry about it.

And the next warning I had was about 5 after 8, when we received a call that there was an attack on.

23. General FRANK. What did you assume this was that was coming in? It might have been what?

Colonel TYLER. As far as I was concerned, it could. I thought it most probable that it would be the B-17's which were coming from the mainland.

24. General FRANK. You knew there was a flight of B-17s due in?

Colonel TYLER. I didn't have official information. You see, I had a friend who was a bomber pilot, and he told me, any time that they play this Hawaiian music all night long, it is a very good indication that our B-17s were coming over from the mainland, because they use it for homing; and when I had reported for duty at 4 o'clock

in the morning, I listened to this Hawaiian music all the
way into town, and so I figured then that we had a flight
of B-17s coming in; so that came to my mind as soon as I
got this call from him.

25. General FRANK. Did you give any thought to the
fact that it might be planes from a navy carrier?

Colonel TYLER. Yes, sir. In fact, I thought that was
just about an equal probability of the two.

26. General FRANK. What did you do, from then on?

Colonel TYLER. Well, there was nothing to do between the call, until the attack came.

27. General FRANK. Where were you when the attack came?

Colonel TYLER. I was awaiting relief. I was due at
8 o'clock to be relieved, and there being nothing going
on, I just stepped outside of the door. There was an outside door, there, and I got a breath of fresh air, and I
actually saw the planes coming down on Pearl Harbor;
but even then, I thought they were Navy planes; and I
saw antiaircraft shooting, which I thought was practicing
antiaircraft.

28. General FRANK. The last connection that you
had with this station was when you told the operator up
at Opana to "forget it," so to speak?

Colonel TYLER. Yes, sir.

29. General RUSSELL. How long had you been in the
Air Corps, then, Colonel?

Colonel TYLER. I was first commissioned in 1937.
I had it, just a little over four years, sir, at that time.

30. General RUSSELL. You knew something about
the mission of fighter airplanes, did you?

Colonel TYLER. Yes, sir.

31. General RUSSELL. And you knew that the pursuit officer in that information center was there to get
planes in the air, to intercept incoming hostile planes if
they appeared, did you?

Colonel TYLER. Yes, sir.

32. General RUSSELL. And you knew the only thing you had to do was to get in touch with the people who could put those planes up, isn't that true?

Colonel TYLER. That is not exactly true, sir, because we had nothing on the alert. We had no planes.

33. General RUSSELL. Well, if you had had some planes on the alert, then your job was to call for the commander of those planes and tell him, "Here come some enemy planes—go get them!" Wasn't that your job as the pursuit officer?

Colonel TYLER. That would be my job if I had any way of telling. There was no means of identifying.

34. General RUSSELL. There seemed to be a lot of mystery about a pursuit officer and your not being trained as a pursuit officer, and I am trying to see if I can solve that mystery. You had a telephone in that place, on which you could talk to the commanders of the aircraft on the Islands?

Colonel TYLER. Well, my next higher, the first one there called would have been Major Bergquist. I would have called him in his quarters, I presume.

35. General RUSSELL. Then he was to tell the people to get into the planes and go get the enemy?

Colonel TYLER. That was his duty; yes, sir.

36. General RUSSELL. So it was a rather simple job, after all, wasn't it, Colonel?

Colonel TYLER. That's right; it would have been.

37. General RUSSELL. The only mystery about it was the fact that you did not know that there were any Jap planes coming in, there?

Colonel TYLER. Yes, sir.

38. General RUSSELL. And you had the information from this boy at the Opana radar station that he had picked up the biggest flight that he had ever picked up, is that right?

Colonel TYLER. Yes, sir.

39. General RUSSELL. Did he appear somewhat excited over the flight that was coming in?

Colonel TYLER. I would say that he seemed more than normal. Of course, I didn't know the fellow up there, but he seemed—I would say he was interested in it, all right, sir.

40. General RUSSELL. He had found something out there, that had impressed him to quite an extent?

Colonel TYLER. Yes, sir.

41. General RUSSELL. And you said, "Don't worry about it—don't bother"? That was your decision, is that right?

Colonel TYLER. Yes, sir.

AMBASSADOR OSHIMA'S CONVERSATION WITH VON RIBBENTROP, NOVEMBER 28, 1941[30]

The following intercept of a report of a conversation between Japanese Ambassador Hiroshi Oshima and Joachim von Ribbentrop gave an indication of Germany's stiffening attitude toward American entry into the war. (Parts 2 and 3 omitted).

γ   γ   γ

[Secret]

From: Berlin
To: Tokyo
29 November 1941
(Purple)
#1393   (In 3 parts, complete)

By his request, I was supposed to have called on Foreign Minister Ribbentrop during the evening of yesterday, the 28th. Suddenly, however, he requested that the time be postponed and it was not until 10:30 at night that I finally saw him.

This delay was occasioned by the fact that a long conference of the bigwigs of the government and military from Goering down, was being held at the official residence of the Fuehrer. The war against the Soviet Union has now taken definite shape and the outcome can be unerringly foretold. Next year's campaigns were mapped at this conference, taking into consideration the points brought up at the conference of the various Prime Ministers and Foreign Ministers of Europe. It is an absolute certainty that Japan's moves were also given discussion at this conference.

1. Ribbentrop opened our meeting by again inquiring whether I had received any reports regarding the Japanese-U.S. negotiations. I replied that I had received no official word.

[30]*Pearl Harbor Attack*, Part XII, 200.

Ribbentrop: "It is essential that Japan effect the New Order in East Asia without losing this opportunity. There never has been and probably never will be a time when closer cooperation under the Tripartite Pact is so important. If Japan hesitates at this time, and Germany goes ahead and establishes her European New Order, all the military might of Britain and the United States will be concentrated against Japan.

"As Fuehrer Hitler said today, there are fundamental differences in the very right to exist between Germany and Japan, and the United States. We have received advice to the effect that there is practically no hope of the Japanese-U.S. negotiations being concluded successfully, because of the fact that the United States is putting up a stiff front.

"If this is indeed the fact of the case, and if Japan reaches a decision to fight Britain and the United States, I am confident that that will not only be to the interest of Germany and Japan jointly, but would bring about favorable results for Japan herself."

I: "I can make no definite statement as I am not aware of any concrete intentions of Japan. Is Your Excellency indicating that a state of actual war is to be established between Germany and the United States?"

Ribbentrop: "Roosevelt's a fanatic, so it is impossible to tell what he would do."

Concerning this point, in view of the fact that Ribbentrop has said in the past that the United States would undoubtedly try to avoid meeting German troops, and from the tone of Hitler's recent speech as well as that of Ribbentrop's, I feel that German attitude toward the United States is being considerably stiffened. There are indications at present that Germany would not refuse to fight the United States if necessary. . . .

JAPANESE WAR WARNING TO GERMANY, NOVEMBER 30, 1941[31]

The following instructions from Tokyo to the Japanese Ambassador in Berlin, which were intercepted by Magic, were a clear indication of the imminence of war.

γ γ γ

[Secret]

From: Tokyo
To: Berlin
November 30, 1941
Purple (CA)
#985. (Part 1 of 3)

Re my Circular #2387.

1. The conversations begun between Tokyo and Washington last April during the administration of the former cabinet, in spite of the sincere efforts of the Imperial Government, now stand ruptured—broken. (I am sending you an outline of developments in separate message #986) In the face of this, our Empire faces a grave situation and must act with determination. Will Your Honor, therefore, immediately interview Chancellor **HITLER** and Foreign Minister **RIBBENTROP** and confidentially communicate to them a summary of the developments. Say to them that lately England and the United States have taken a provocative attitude, both of them. Say that they are planning to move military forces into various places in East Asia and that we will inevitably have to counter by also moving troops. Say very secretly to them that there is extreme danger that war may suddenly break out between the Anglo-Saxon nations and Japan through some clash of arms and add that the time of the breaking out of this war may come quicker than anyone dreams.

Army 25552
JD: 6943 Trans. 12-1-41 (NR)

[31] *Pearl Harbor Attack,* Part XII, p. 204

BIBLIOGRAPHY

Bailey, Thomas A., and Ryan, Paul B., *Hitler vs. Roosevelt: The Undeclared Naval War* (New York: Free Press, 1979).

Baker, Leonard, *Roosevelt and Pearl Harbor* (New York: Macmillan, 1970.)

Barnes, Harry Elmer, *Pearl Harbor After a Quarter of a Century* (New York: Arno Press, 1972).

Barnes, Harry Elmer, ed., *Perpetual War for Perpetual Peace: A Critical Examination of the Foreign Policy of Franklin Delano Roosevelt and Its Aftermath* (Caldwell, Idaho: Caxton, 1953).

Barron, Gloria J., *Leadership in Crisis: Franklin D. Roosevelt and the Path to Intervention* (Port Washington: Kennikat, 1973).

Bartlett, Bruce R., *Cover-Up: The Politics of Pearl Harbor, 1941-1946* (New Rochelle: Arlington House, 1978).

Beard, Charles A., *President Roosevelt and the Coming of the War, 1941: A Study in Appearances and Realities* (New Haven: Yale Univ. Press, 1948).

Bergamini, David, *Japan's Imperial Conspiracy: How Emperor Hirohito led Japan into war against the West* (New York: William Morrow, 1971).

Borg, Dorothy, and Okamoto, Shumpei, eds., *Pearl Harbor as History: Japanese-American Relations, 1936-1941* (New York: Columbia Univ. Press, 1973).

Brownlow, Donald Grey, *The Accused: The Ordeal of Rear Admiral Husband Edward Kimmel, U.S.N.* (New York: Vantage, 1968).

Burns, James MacGregor, *Roosevelt: The Soldier of Freedom* (New York: Harcourt, Brace Javanovich, 1970).

Burtness, Paul S. and Ober, Warren J., eds., *The Puzzle of Pearl Harbor* (Evanston, Ill.: Thorp, Peterson, 1962).

Butow, Robert J.C. "The Hull-Nomura Conversations: A Fundamental Misconception," *Am. Hist. Review,* LXV (July 1960), 822-36.

Butow, Robert J.C., *Tojo and the Coming of the War* (Princeton: Princeton Univ. Press, 1961).

Chomsky, Noam, *American Power and the New Mandarins* (New York: Pantheon, 1967).

Cole, Wayne S., "American Entry Into World War II: A Historiographical Appraisal," *Mississippi Valley Historical Review,* XLIII (1957), 595-617.

Crowley, James G., "A New Deal for Japan and Asia: One Road to Pearl Harbor," in James B. Crowley, ed., *Modern East Asia: Essays in Interpretation* (New York: Harcourt, Brace, 1970), 235-64.

Current, Richard N., *Secretary Stimson: A Study in Statecraft* (New Brusnwick, N.J.: Rutgers Univ. Press, 1954).

Dallek, Robert, *Franklin D. Roosevelt and American Foreign Policy, 1932-1945* (New York: Oxford Univ. Press, 1979).

Divine, Robert A., *The Reluctant Belligerent: American Entry into World War II* (New York: Wiley, 1965).

Doenecke, Justus D., "Beyond Polemics: An Historiographical Reappraisal of American Entry into World War II," *History Teacher* (1979), 217-51.

Farago, Ladislas, *The Broken Seal: The Story of "Operation Magic" and the Pearl Harbor Disaster* (New York: Random House, 1967).

Fehrenbach, T.R., *F.D.R's Undeclared War, 1939-1941* (New York: David McKay, 1967).

Feis, Herbert, *The Road to Pearl Harbor: The Coming of the War Between the United States and Japan* (Princeton: Princeton Univ. Press, 1950).

Ferrell, Robert H., "Pearl Harbor and the Revisionists," *Historian,* XVII (1955), 215-33.

Flynn, John T., *The Truth About Pearl Harbor* (New York: John T. Flynn, 1944).

Fuchida, Matsuo, and Okumiya, Masatake, *Midway: The Battle That Doomed Japan: The Japanese Navy's Story* (Annapolis: U.S. Naval Institute, 1955.)

Fukudome, Shigeru, "Hawaii Operation," *U.S. Naval Institute Proceedings,* LXXXI (December 1955), 1315-31.

Grew, Joseph C., *Ten Years in Japan: A Contemporary Record Drawn from the Diaries and Private and Official Papers of Joseph C. Grew, United States Ambassador to Japan, 1932-1942* (New York: Simon & Schuster, 1944).

Herde, Peter, *7. Dezember 1941: Der Ausbruch des Krieges zwischen Japan und den Vereinigten Staaten und die Ausweitung des europäischen Krieges zum Zweiten Weltkrieg.* Impulse der Forschung, Band 33 (Darmstadt: Wissenschaftliche Buchgesellschaft, 1980).

Herzog, James H., *Closing the Open Door: American-Japanese Diplomatic Negotiations, 1936-1941* (Annapolis: Naval Institute Press, 1973).

Higgins, Trumbull, "East Wind Rain," *United States Naval Institute Proceedings,* LXXXI (November 1955), 1198-1203.

Hoehling, A.A., *America's Road to War: 1939-1941* (London: Abelard-Schuman, 1970).

Hoehling, A.A., *The Week Before Pearl Harbor* (New York: Norton, 1963).

Hull, Cordell, *The Memoirs of Cordell Hull* (New York: Macmillan, 1957).

Ike, Nobutaka, *Japan's Decision for War: Records of the 1941 Policy Conferences* (Stanford: Stanford Univ. Press, 1967).

Kato, Masuo, *The Lost War: A Japanese Reporter's Inside Story* (New York: Knopf, 1946).

Kimmel, Husband E., *Admiral Kimmel's Story* (Chicago: Henry Regnery, 1955).

Langer, William L., and Gleason, S. Everett, *The Undeclared War, 1940-1941* (New York: Harper, 1953).

Lord, Walter, *Day of Infamy* (New York: Holt, 1957).

Lu, David J., *From the Marco Polo Bridge to Pearl Harbor: Japan's Entry into World War II* (Washington: Public Affairs Press, 1961).

McKechney, John, "The Pearl Harbor Controversy: A Debate Among Historians," *Monumenta Nipponica*, XVIII (1963), 44-87.

Melosi, Martin V., *The Shadow of Pearl Harbor: Political Controversy over the Surprise Attack, 1941-1946* (College Station: Texas A&M Univ. Press, 1977).

Morgenstern, George, *Pearl Harbor: The Story of the Secret War* (New York: Devin-Adair, 1947).

Morison, Elting E., *Turmoil and Tradition: A Study of the Life and Times of Henry L. Stimson* (Cambridge: Houghton, Mifflin, 1960).

Morison, Samuel Eliot, "Did Roosevelt Start the War? History Through a Beard," *Atlantic Monthly*, CLXXXII (August 1948), 91-97.

Morison, Samuel Eliot, *The Two Ocean War: A Short History of the United States Navy in the Second World War* (Boston: Little, Brown, 1963).

Morton, Louis, "Pearl Harbor in Perspective: A Bibliographical Survey," *U.S. Naval Institute Proceedings*, LXXXI (April 1953), 461-68.

Neumann, William, *The Genesis of Pearl Harbor* (Philadelphia: Pacifist Research Bureau, 1945).

Okumiya, Masatake, and Horikoshi, Jiro (with Martin Caidin), *Zero* (New York: Dutton, 1956).

Parkinson, Roger, *Attack on Pearl Harbor* (London: Wayland, 1973).

Perkins, Frances, *The Roosevelt I Knew* (New York: Viking, 1946).

Picker, Heinrich, ed., *Hitlers Tischgespräche im Führerhauptquartier, 1941-42* (Bonn: Athenäum, 1951).

Pogue, Forest, *George C. Marshall: Ordeal and Hope, 1939-1942* (New York: Viking, 1966).

Potter, John Dean, *Yamamoto, The Man Who Menaced America* (New York: Viking, 1965).

Prange, Gordon W. *At Dawn We Slept: The Untold Story of Pearl Harbor* (New York McGraw-Hill, 1981).

Russett, Bruce, *No Clear and Present Danger: The U.S. Entry into World War II* (New York: Harper, 1972).

Sanborn, Frederick, *Design for War: A Study of Secret Power Politics, 1937-1941* (New York: Devin-Adair, 1951).

Schmidt, Paul, *Statist of diplomatischer Bühne, 1923-45* (Bonn: Athenäum, 1949).

Schroeder, Paul W., *The Axis Alliance and Japanese-American Relations 1941* (Ithaca: Cornell Univ. Press, 1958).

Stimson, Henry L., and Bundy, McGeorge, *On Active Service in Peace and War* (New York: Harper, 1948).

Tansill, Charles Callan, *Back Door to War: The Roosevelt Foreign Policy, 1933-1941* (Chicago: Henry Regnery, 1952).

Theobald, Robert A., *The Final Secret of Pearl Harbor: The Washington Contribution to the Japanese Attack* (New York: Devin-Adair, 1954).

Thürk, Harry, *Pearl Harbor: Die Geschichte eines Überfalls* (n.d., n.p.)

Togo, Shigenori, *The Cause of Japan* (New York: Simon & Schuster, 1956).

Toland, John, *But Not In Shame: The Six Months After Pearl Harbor* (New York: Random House, 1961).

Tolley, Kemp, *Cruise of the Lanikai: Incitement to War* (Annapolist: Naval Institute Press, 1973).

Trefousse, Hans L., *Germany and American Neutrality, 1939-1941* (New York: Bookman, 1951).

Trefousse, Hans L. *What Happened at Pearl Harbor?* (New York: Twayne, 1957).

U.S. Congress, 79th Cong., 2d Sess., *Investigation of the Pearl Harbor Attack: Report of the Joint Committee on the Investigation of the Pearl Harbor Attack,* Sen. Doc. No. 244 (Washington, 1946).

Wallin, Homer N., *Pearl Harbor: Why, How, Fleet Salvage and Final Appraisal* (Washington: Government Printing Office, 1968).

Weinberg, Gerhard L., "Germany's Declaration of War on the United States: A New Look, " in Hans L. Trefousse, ed., *Germany and America: Essays on Problems of International Relations and Immigration* (New York: Brooklyn College Press, 1980), 54-70.

Weinberg, Gerhard L., "Hitler's Image of the United States," *American Historical Review,* LXIX (July 1964), 1006-21.

Wiltz, John E., *From Isolation to War, 1931-1941* (New York: Crowell, 1968).

Wohlstetter, Roberta, *Pearl Harbor: Warning and Decision* (Stanford: Stanford Univ. Press, 1962).

Yoshikawa, Takeo (with Norman Stanford), "Top Secret Assignment," *U.S. Naval Institute Proceedings,* LXXXVI (December 1960), 27-39.

INDEX

211